The 88 Temples of Shikoku
Walking 88 Temples in 55 Days

Second edition
© 2024 Oliver Dunskus
Verlag: BoD · Books on Demand GmbH, In de Tarpen 42,
22848 Norderstedt
Druck: Libri Plureos GmbH, Friedensallee 273,
22763 Hamburg
ISBN: 978-3-7693-1914-9

Preface

This guide is intended to be used in connection with *The 88 Temples of Shikoku, a Guide for the Walking Pilgrim* by the same author.

While my regular guidebook describes all the temples and walking parts in detail, this guide offers a concept on how to walk the 88 temples in 55 days in an optimal way, in ideal stages between 15 and, where necessary, 34 km per day considering topography, sightseeing and infrastructure. Following this guide, the pilgrimage would be done in 55 days not including resting days.

Today, staying at guesthouses is the common way to do the pilgrimage. Sleeping outside or in huts or free-of-charge temple shelters (Shukubo) is not an option which I recommend, and it should be considered only if there is no other option.

A break of at least 30 minutes per temple is a good amount of time to include. It will allow us to visit the premises, chant the Heart Sutra, have a drink, visit the washroom and queue for our stamp without being under pressure. Some smaller temples can be visited in shorter time, if necessary, but it is always good to include some resting time for yourself, or some time for a chat with priests or fellow pilgrims, as the interaction with locals or other pilgrims is one of the many pleasures of the pilgrimage, and it may be unplanned and spontaneous.

As the entire pilgrimage along the 88 main temples covers a length of 1137 km, 55 days represents an average of about 21 km per day, rest days not included.

The KM (Full Kilometer) indications refer to the maps shown in the *Shikoku Japan 88 Route Guide* by Naoyuki Matsushita, 2024 edition (Buyodo Co. Ltd.) which is the best map-book for the pilgrimage. It displays the overall kilometers along the official route in blue every 5 km and contains much other helpful information.

The indications about public transportation are incomplete and just included for emergency purposes in remote areas.

If I wanted to walk the Shikoku pilgrimage again, knowing what I know today and just focusing on the 88 temples, this book shows how I would plan my days.

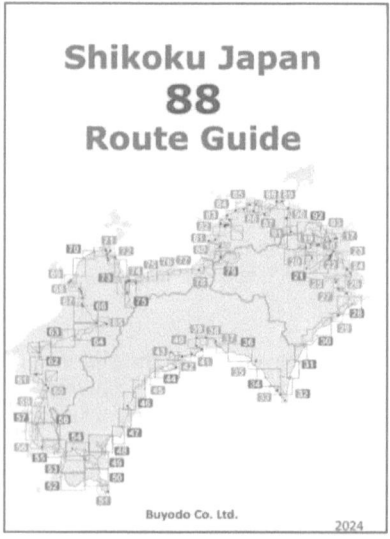

*Shikoku Japan 88
Route Guide map book*

*The 88 Temples of Shikoku
guidebook*

Symbols

⛩	Shinto Shrines (selected)
🚉	Train Stations (selected)
🚌	Bus stops (selected)
🚠	Ropeway
🍴	Restaurant or Coffee Shop (outside cities)
🚻	Toilets all temples and many shrines have toilets
🛏	Accommodations (selected)
⛺	Camping Site
🛒	Convenience store or supermarket (outside cities)
T1	Official Temple with Number (One of the 88 Main Temples)
B1	Bekkaku Temple (One of the 20 Separate *Bekkaku* Temples) with Number
O1	Inner Sanctuary or Sacred Places related to Temple
KM	Full Km Position according to the *Shikoku Japan 88 Route Guide* 2024 edition (White numbers in blue square)
Daily Km	Km per day
X	Crossing
△	Peak, pass, highest point of climb
↗	Moderate climb (up to 10% or 100 m per km)
↗↗	Challenging Climb (above 10% or 100 m per km)
↘	Moderate Gradient (below 10% or 100 m per km)
↘↘	Steep Gradient (above 10% or 100 m per km)

Day 0 - Arrival in Tokushima	
Distance	0
Km	0
⚞	Tokushima has plenty of hotels in all categories.
	Some recommendations:
	Henro House Aruki Henro Yado, Hostel PAQ

Although Tokushima hosts none of the official 88 temples, it is a good starting point for the pilgrimage and the perfect place to meet fellow pilgrims coming from other locations to begin the pilgrimage together. It is easily accessible by train, by car from the Kansai region, or by long distance bus from Osaka, Kyoto or Kansai Airport. You can take the bus either to Tokushima (central station) which is another 20 minutes by train from T1, or to the highway bus station Naruto Nishi 鳴門西 on the long-distance bus from Osaka to Takamatsu

There are plenty of hotels and restaurants near the main station. If time permits, the arrival day can be spent visiting Mount Bizan by ropeway and enjoying the panorama from this mythical mountain top. Next to the ropeway we have Odori-Kaikan, an event center for the regional dance tradition, which has a large souvenir shop located on the ground floor which also sells basic pilgrimage gear. As you may find other options along the way, you may limit yourself to just buying the stamp book, some candles an incense-sticks, the most important things to bring when visiting temple 1 the next day.

I also strongly recommend to buy the Shikoku Japan 88 Route Guide, which is available at the tourist center in the ground floor of the department store opposite Tokushima Station, ask for Lance Kita. Or even better – get it while you are still preparing your trip.

Tokushima will be the only major city for the next two weeks. Should you need some hiking gear, Montbell is a good place for final provisions, but it is located 10 km NW outside the city. Check Google Maps for the best suitable public transportation.

Day 1: T1 to T6 - The Start (by Train to Bando)

Distance	17 km:
KM	KM 0 to KM 16
🛏	T6 Guesthouse or T7 Guesthouse, 2 km further

Our first stage is a perfect to warm-up. After taking the Kotoku Line to Bando, we will visit six temples. The pilgrimage begins gently and with no hills. The walk takes about 8.5 hours. Assuming we begin our day at Tokushima Station at 8 a.m. taking the train to Bando, and including a visit to the pilgrimage shop at T1, we would be done at 5 pm, arriving at our guesthouse appr. 1 hour before sunset. Make sure to check in before 6 pm. There are some more sites that may be included on our first day:

- Oasahiko-Shrine, impressive Shinto shrine near T1. Add 2 km , 1 h
- The German House Naruto, a museum about the German prisoners of war in WWI. Add 1 hour, no major detour
- Temple B1 Taisan-ji. Impressive temple located in the mountains. Add 8 km and 4 hours. In this case, it is recommendable to spend the night already near T5 (Henro-House Morimotoya) and to include the missing stage T5-T6 (5km/1h) the next day. This (T1-T5 and B1) would turn our first day into a feasible hike of 20 km and 10-11 hours.

KM	Daily km	Point of Interest
0	0	**T1 Ryozen-ji,** detour to ⛩Oasahiko
1	1	**T2 Gokuraku-ji**
2	2	� Awa-Kawabata, Naruto German House
3	3	🛒
4	4	**T3 Konsen-ji**
5	5	🚌 Itano
6	6	Hokoku-ji, huge camphor tree
7	7	🛒 ⛩Suwa
8	8	O3 Aizen-In, nice place to take a rest
9	9	🍲 Aizome-an, **T4 Dainichi-ji**
10	10	🛏 hut
11	11	O5 Rakan, **T5 Jizo-ji** 🛒
12	12	🚌 Rakan
13	13	Henro-goya hut No. 44, 🍲 Udon, 🛒
		Beginning of detour to **B1Dainichi-ji** (10 km)
14	14	🚌 Kanyake
15	15	Hozoji Temple
16	16	🚌 Higashihara, end of detour from B1
		T6 Anraku-ji

Day 2: T7 to T10 and Crossing Yoshino River	
Distance	20 km (depending on where we sleep):
KM	KM 18 to Km 38
🛏	Awaraku-ya (KM 34)
	Channel-Kan in Kamojima (off KM 35)
	Oyado Eleven near T11 (KM 38)

While our first day was mostly flat, our second day will give us a first taste of walking uphill. Until T7, the walk is flat and unspectacular.

The way to Temple 8 is 100 m uphill. You have not arrived yet when you see the huge gate next to the highway, the temple is slightly further uphill. Take a little more time for this one as the place is beautiful but spread over a larger area.

Downhill again to Temple 9, and its little restaurant might be a good place for an early lunch.

It will take one hour to continue to Temple 10. On the way we will pass Sumotori-ya, one of the best shops for pilgrimage gear and souvenirs, it is located on the way up, just under the expressway, the last shop of the village. When we finally made it, we need to climb another 333 steps, to reach the main building situated at 157 m altitude. The temple's okunoin Hasso-Daishi is another 50 m up. On stretches like the ramps to T10, where the road is paved and steep, but with very little circulation, you can rest your aching muscles by occasionally walking uphill backwards. You will be surprised at how good the front muscles of your upper thighs can do the job.

There is a nice Udon-Restaurant called Udon-tei just 2 km after leaving T10.

The last one and a half days we have been walking along the north side of the Yoshino-river valley. The last part for the day will now be to cross the river to the other side. There are two bridges: Awa-Chuo bridge on the east is a steel bridge for the heavy traffic, leading straight to the town of Kamojima. Kawajima bridge is a narrow submersible bridge for lighter cars and pedestrians, and we will pass beautiful riverbed landscapes on the way. This one is the nicer choice, as we head for one of the guesthouses in Awa-City or Yoshinogawa, or we continue to the new hostel next to T11.

KM	Daily km	Point of Interest
16	0	**T6 Anraku-ji**
17	1	⛩ Kumano
18	2	**T7 Juraku-ji** 🍴
19	3	Marker, Bridge over Miyagochi-Tani-River
20	4	Police X Highway 318 to Yoshinogawa
21	5	Hiramizu Daishi, Henro-goya hut No. 57, 500 m to Onsen 🍴
22	6	**Gate, T8 Kumadani-ji**
23	7	
24	8	**T9 Horinji (** 🚌 1.5 km**)**
25	9	🍴 Awaji-An, Shonen-ji Temple
26	10	Azukiara Daishi, Horon-ji
27	11	
28	12	↗↗ Sumotori-Ya (Pilgrimage gear shop), **T10 Kirihata-ji** △
29	13	↘↘
30	14	X Highway 12, Henro-goya hut no. 45 🍴 Udon-Tei
31	15	🈶 ⛩ Hachiman-gu
32	16	Onojima bridge
33	17	Zennyujima Island
34	18	Kawashima bridge, 🛏 Awaraku-ya
35	19	
36	20	Awa-Town,
37	21	🚉 2 km to Kamojima Station
38	22	🛏 ⛺ Oyado Eleven

The two-story Henro-goya hut no. 45, at KM 30

Day 3: T11 and T12 - Heavy Duty	
Distance	17 km, appr. 1,200 m climbs (Challenge)
KM	KM 36 to KM 53
🛏	Sudachi-an KM 53, Moja-House KM 57 or several options in Kamiyama

On our third day, we will face one of the hardest stages of the pilgrimage. But don't worry, this is not the Himalayas.

The hike begins with a few km to T11, from there it is mostly uphill across the forest, and it takes 6 to 7 hours in total to reach Sudachi-an, the first guesthouse after T12. We will pass our first "henro korogashi" stretch, this is the name for particularly tough or steep parts of the pilgrimage. The 11 km from T11 to T12 are entirely on forest trails and steps. But it is not over when reaching T12.

<u>Take enough food and drinks for two days</u>, as there are absolutely no shops or even vending machines except at the temples. There will also be no stores the next day for the first 18 km. T12 does not offer accommodation. There is just one place to stay near T12, Sudachi-an, make sure it is available, as the remaining guesthouses are temporarily or currently closed. Water is possibly available on the route after 5 km at the fountain and after 10 km at Joren-an.

In case it all goes wrong and you are afraid to get stuck in the mountains after T12, follow route 43 downhill 4 km to the town of Kamiyama, where you will find more guesthouses or a bus connection to Tokushima. You can also stay in Tokushima and return to Kamiyama the next morning and continue where you finished the day before.

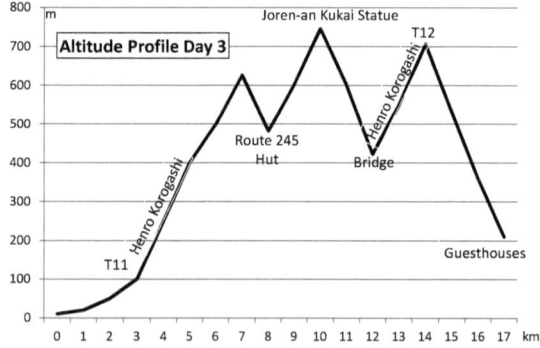

KM	Daily km	Point of Interest
36	0	🚃 🚌 Kamojima-town or Awa-town
37	1	
38	2	Hut, 1 km to Kamo-no-yu public bath
39	3	**T11 Fuji-dera** (100 m)
40	4	↗↗ Henro Korogashi
41	5	↗↗ Chodo-an (400 m)
42	6	↗↗
43	7	△ (626 m)
44	8	↘↘ Valley, O12 Ryusui-an (482 m) Tap water
45	9	↗↗
46	10	↗↗ O12 Joren-an, hut, 🏕, △ (745 m)
47	11	↘↘
48	12	↘↘ Deep valley, bridge (422 m)
49	13	↗↗ Henro Korogashi
50	14	**T12 Shosan-ji** (706 m) △
51	15	↘↘
52	16	O12 Joshin-an
53	17	↘🛏 Sudachi-an (210 m), 3 km to Moja House or several options in Kamiyama

T12 Shosan-ji protected by cedar trees of up to 50 m height

Day 4: T13 to T17 and back to Tokushima City	
Distance	34 km
KM	KM 53 - KM 87
🛏	Tokushima

After yesterday's challenge, today's walk is long but mostly downhill without major challenges, as we return to Tokushima.

In the morning we have 4 to 5 hours across remote areas along a river until we reach T13. Just before T13 we will pass the first convenience store of the day.

This is followed by a series of five temples. After T17 it is time to reach our place to stay for the night, preferably in the center of Tokushima, where we might also give our legs a treat in a hot bath (These are called Sento).

In case 34 km is too much, we can take finish the day by train from Kou station 1 km south of T17, skipping the last 6 km. There are not many places to stay between Tokushima and T18, so the city is a good place to spend the night.

B2 is well worth a detour, it would be just 2 km more. After 13 km take the north side of the river. All in all, it might be worthwhile to include B2 and to take the train to Tokushima from Kou – it would be a temple more and 4 km less, but still be a 30 km hike to be proud of.

Hasso Daishi at KM 75

14

KM	Daily km	Point of Interest
53	0	🛏 Sudachi-an (210 m), after 300 m go left on the trail
54	1	↗↗
55	2	↗↗ △ Tamaga Pass (450 m), ⓘ
56	3	↘ Henro-goya hut no.36
57	4	↘ 1 km to Moja House
58	5	↘
59	6	↘
60	7	🚌 ⓘ Bridge, 🛏 Uemura Guesthouse
61	8	
62	9	
63	10	
64	11	🚌 Hirono ⛩ Akiba 🛒
65	12	
66	13	Bridge. For B2, walk northern riverside
67	14	
68	15	Detour to **B2 Dogaku-ji** (4 km)
69	16	
70	17	ⓘ, Bridge, Hut 🍴 Komorebi Cafe
71	18	Bridge 🛒 ⛺
72	19	**T13 Dainichi-ji**, 🚌
73	20	Ichinomiya Bridge
74	21	**T14 Joraku-ji,** O14 Jigenji
75	22	Hasso-daishi, **T15 Kokubun-ji**
76	23	🍴 Hanamaru Udon (1 block to the right)
77	24	**T16 Kannon-ji** 🍴 Namata Soba
78	25	🛒, ⛩ Omiwa, 🛒 🛏 Uroko-ro
79	26	🚈 Kou
80	27	**T17 Ido-ji**
81	28	
82	29	
83	30	🛒 🛒
84	31	🚈 Akui 🛒 ⓘ
85	32	🚈 Kuramoto
86	33	🛒 ⓘ
87	34	🚈 🚌 Tokushima central Station

Day 5: T18 and T19 - Leaving the City

Distance	18.7 km
KM	KM 87 - KM 106
🛏	Henro-House Fun Farm or T19 Guesthouse

After the strenuous last two days, we will afford a shorter stage which is easy to find and mostly flat. The first monotonous 10 km are along Highway 55 which takes out of the city. The recommended stay is 2-3 km after T19. This stage should not take more than 6 hours, so we can sleep longer before we go but we need to be on the road by 11 am.

KM	Daily km	Point of Interest
87	0	🚉 Tokushima central
88	1	
89	2	🛒
90	3	
91	4	🛒 🍽 Several Restaurants, Bridge over Sonose River
92	5	
93	6	
94	7	Katsuura Bridge
95	8	🚉 Chuden, hut
96	9	🍽 🛒
97	10	Follow the smaller road into the hills
98	11	🚌 Onzanji-mae
99	12	**T18 Onzan-ji**
100	13	
101	14	🛒
102	15	Okyozuka temple, hut
103	16	Bridge **T19 Tatsue-ji**
104	17	🍽 Kohaku no tenshi
105	18	
106	19	⛩ Tenma, 🛏 Henro-House Fun-Farm

Day 6: T20 and T21 - Two Tough Beauties	
Distance	16 km, 1,000 m climbs (Challenge)
KM	KM 106 to KM 122
🛏	Iyashi-tei Koku (KM 122, Ropeway to T21) or several options near T22, (several options)

16 km may sound like a moderate distance for the day, but the two climbs involved are of 500 m each, both containing a henro korogashi stretch. Make sure to have enough supplies of food and water when heading into the mountains after the Hina-no-sato road station at KM 113. The entire stage should take about 7 hours including the temple visits. Take your time for these two temples, they are beautiful. Optionally, you can add 10 km and stay near T22, reducing the stage of the next day.

Again, make sure to <u>carry enough food and drink for 2 days</u> as there will be no shops or restaurants between Km 113 and Km 152.

Iyashi-tei, the guesthouse at the river next to the ropeway station to T21 is the only accommodation in the area. If you do not feel like doing two heavy climbs in one day, after getting down from T20 turn right at KM 118 when you get to the bridge and follow the river for appr. 7 km to the guesthouse. The next morning you can take the ropeway up to T21 and continue as planned.

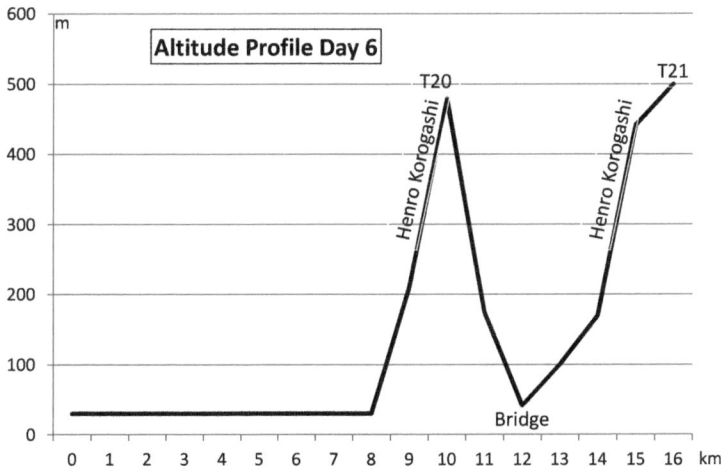

KM	Daily km	Point of Interest
106	0	⛩Hachiman
107	1	🏯Hosenji
108	2	
109	3	⛩ 🛒
110	4	
111	5	🍽 Aoki Shokudo
112	6	Detour to Hoshino-Iwaya waterfalls
113	7	🍽 Hina-no-sato road station, shops, 🏯, 🛒 (Last shop for the next 50 km/2 days) 🚌 Ikuna 🏯 detour to B3 begins here
114	8	↗↗ 🏯 hut
115	9	↗↗Henro-Korogashi
116	10	**T20 Kakurin-ji** △ (494 m) ↘↘
117	11	↘↘
118	12	↘↘ 🏯 hut, Bridge over Naka-river (42 m),
119	13	↘↘ follow the river to the right to go directly to Iyashi-tei guesthouse ↗↗
120	14	↗↗ hut 🏯
121	15	↗↗Henro-Korogashi
122	16	**T21 Tairyu-ji** △ (500 m) 🚠 down to 🛏 Iyashi-tei Koku

The ropeway connecting Naka-river with T21, covers 450 m of altitude

Day 7: T22 and T23 - To the Coast	
Distance	31 km
KM	KM 122 to KM 153
🛏	Several options in Hiwasa: Ichi-the-hostel, or guesthouse Oyado Hiwasa and others

Take along enough food and drink for the day.

After yesterday's short but hard stage, this one is long, but after visiting the panoramic southern Shashin, it goes mostly downhill until we reach T22 after 11 km.

We will follow Route 55 across the mountains until we reach the city of Hiwasa, the train station, the highway rest area and T23 Yakuoji.

Just before reaching T23, we will finally catch a first glimpse of the sea, for the first time during our pilgrimage, but it will take another 17 km until the route finally heads along the coast and that will be during the next day.

T23 is an interesting temple in a beautiful location overlooking the coast, take some time to discover it. No need to hurry up, in case we get there too late we can visit it the next morning, our next stage will be short.

Should this distance be too short, you can take the train all the way to Hiwasa and T23 from either Aratano which is at KM 11, 1.2 km from T22, or from Awa-fukui at KM 16.

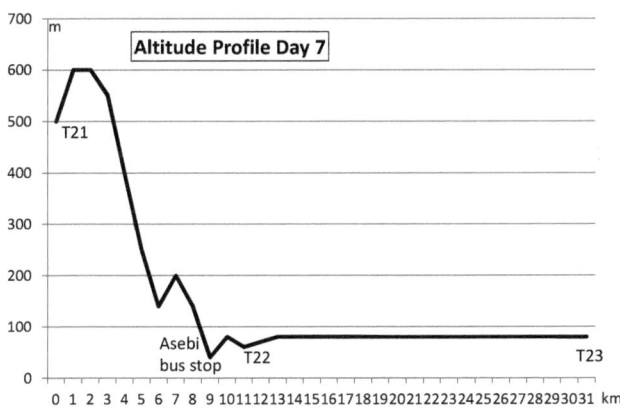

19

KM	Daily km	Point of Interest
122	0	**T21 Tairyu-ji** 🚠 (500 m) up from ⬓ Iyashi-tei Koku
123	1	O21 Shashingatake. South Shashin viewpoint
124	2	↘
125	3	↘
126	4	↘
127	5	↘
128	6	🚌 Asebi (140 m) Henro-goya hut #3
129	7	↗ One-Pass △ (250 m)
130	8	↘
131	9	↘ Henro-goya hut no.47
132	10	Turn left, follow the river
133	11	**T22 Byodo-ji** (38m) 🚂 Aratano and 🍴 1.2 km away
134	12	
135	13	Tsukiyo Omizu Daishi Temple
136	14	Henro-goya hut no.58
137	15	
138	16	🚂 Awa-Fukui, Kane-uchi, Henro-goya hut no. 4
139	17	Turn right on Route 55, O22 Iyadai Kannon, Fukui dam 🚻
140	18	Hut 🚻
141	19	Hut ↘ Hoshigoe tunnel
142	20	↘
143	21	
144	22	🚻 🍴 Café Satsukian
145	23	
146	24	Kubo tunnel, hut
147	25	
148	26	Ichinosaka tunnel
149	27	
150	28	Kaizoku-sen 🍴, 🚻, Henro-goya hut no. 52
151	29	🚂 Kitagawachi
152	30	🍴 4.5 km east: ⛰
153	31	**T23 Yakuo-ji,** 🚂 Hiwasa

Day 8: T23 to T24 Part 1: Sleeping on a Tiny Island	
Distance	15 km to Mugi along Highway 55 across the hills or 20 km to Mugi via Minami Awa Sunline
KM	KM 153 to KM 168 (Mugi)
🛏	Tebajima Guesthouse (Mugi) (former Shanti Guesthouse)

Day 6 has been hard with its climb, and day 7 as well, due to its long distance, so it is time to afford another shorter stage to give our legs a rest. Today we will only walk to Mugi, which will take less than a full day.

Mugi is a good town to stay in. It has a supermarket, convenience stores, a train station (in case things get out of plan) and a beautiful island off the coast called Tebajima, where there is a nice guesthouse called Tebajima Guesthouse (formerly Shanti Guest House). The ship to the island goes five times per day.

In case you feel in good shape and want to go for more, you may also continue on to B4 Saba Daishi (KM 173) and shorten the next day's stage, adding some 5 km to today's stage and stay in one of the guesthouses on the coast.

The main pilgrimage route continues along Route 55 across the hills, one of the less interesting parts of the pilgrimage.

If you want a more interesting alternative, there is a beautiful route from T23 to Mugi called the Awa Sunline, taking us along the coast, walking on a quiet road overlooking the sea. For this one, go left one km after leaving Hiwasa train station. This route avoids the traffic of Route 55 but it also adds 5 km of distance. Once again, there are no food or drink supplies on this route except a vending machine at the first panoramic point after 3 km, so better fill your bottles in Hiwasa before you leave.

There will be no temples today, unless we have kept T23 for this morning.

KM	Daily km	Point of Interest
153	0	T23
154	1	 Hiwasa, 🛒
155	2	Beginning of detour to Mugi along the coast (Minami-Awa Sunline)
156	3	hut, 🚻, Hiwasa tunnel
157	4	
158	5	Henro-goya hut no. 40
159	6	Tunnel, 🚉 Yamagawamachi, 🍽 Odori, 🚻, 🍽 Latorie
160	7	⛩ Yoshino-shrine ⛩ Izumo-shrine
161	8	⛩ Kotohiragu
162	9	Cross the railway, restaurant ruin
163	10	
164	11	↗ Kanba slope ↘
165	12	🚉 Hegawa, Komatsu Daishi, Hut 🚻 🛒
166	13	
167	14	🍽 Wada Bakery
168	15	🚉 Mugi, Ferry to Tebajima, 🛒 🛒

On the way to Tebajima

Day 9: T23 to T24 Part 2 – The End of the Railroad

Distance	25 km
KM	KM 168 to KM 193
🛏	Several options in Ikumi

On our second day from T23 to Cape Muroto and T24, we will visit Bekkaku-temple no. 4 (Saba-Daishi) and see the end of the railroad. The railway company never completed the railway around cape Muroto, KM 190 marks the point where the railroad ends. Public transportation continues by bus for the next 69 km until the railroad resumes from Nahari at KM 259.

If you rely on convenience stores for internet, food supplies, toilets and ATM, be aware that the ones in Awa-Kainan at KM 180 are the last ones for several days until we reach Nahari (KM 259). Make sure you are prepared for 2-3 days without shops. The walk is an easy one along the coast to Ikumi, a village for surfers, which is more or less the last place where we can stay until we get to the cape.

KM	Daily km	Point of Interest
168	0	🚉 Mugi
169	1	
170	2	🚻
171-172	3-4	
173	5	🚉 Sabase, **B4 Saba Daishi**
174	6	
175	7	
176	8	🚉 Asakawa 🚻 🍴 Café Fukunaga, hut
177	9	huts
178	10	
179	11	🚉 Awa-Kainan
180	12	🏪 (last store for 30 km)
181	13	🚉 Kaifu
182-187	14-19	
188	20	🚉 Shishikui, bridge over Shishikui River
189	21	Leaving Tokushima pref., entering Kochi pref.
190	22	🚉, 🚌 Kannoura end of railroad
191	23	
192	24	🚻
193	25	🚌 Ikumi

Day 10: T23 to T24 Part 3 - The Sky and the Sea	
Distance	30 km (Challenge)
KM	KM 193 – KM 223
🛏	Sky and Sea at Km 223, Guesthouse T24

This stage is a mental and physical challenge. It is flat, but monotonous walk across the emptiness along the coast along Highway 55, and you might begin to understand why Kukai might have chosen this location to finally achieve enlightenment in an undisturbed location.

Sakihama, after 17 km, is the only village along the stage which has shops. After 20 lonely kilometers at KM 213, the landscape becomes more interesting with its particular geologic shapes as we can spot the "Couple Rocks" on the coast for the first time. Take along food and drinks on this stage.

I have calculated this stage until KM 223 as this is where infrastructure reappears and we find places to stay. The Cape, and T24 are another 7 km to walk so this will be left for the next day as 30 km are enough.

Should this one become too much of a strain (you would not be the first one to suffer from blisters, thirst, sunburn, loneliness or frustration on this part), the bus passes several times per days and allows you cut it short, it has 39 stops along the route, some are mentioned in the table.

Rock formations at Cape Muroto, near KM 222

24

KM	Daily km	Point of Interest
193	0	🚌 Ikumi Village
194	1	hut
195	2	
196	3	None Village 🚌 Myotokuji (Meitokuji) Temple, 🛈 🚌 Bridge over None River
197	4	
198	5	
199	6	
200	7	🚌 Yodogaiso Bridge
201	8	Hokkaishonindo Temple, 🛈
202	9	
203	10	
204	11	
205	12	Parking, hut
206	13	
207	14	🚌 Yuruki, Bukkai-an Temple, 🛈
208	15	
209	16	⛩ Hachimangu
210	17	🚌 Sakihama 🛒 (Last shop for 25 km) 🛈 🍴 Takosuke
211	18	
212	19	
213	20	🚌 Ozaki Bridge, 🛏 Lodge Ozaki 🛏 Minshuku Tokumasu
214	21	Spotting the "Couple Rocks"
215	22	Meoto Rock, 🍴 Meoto-Iwa Drive-in 🚌 Couple (Husband and Wife) Rocks
216	23	
217	24	
218	25	⛩ Iwata 🛏 Minshuku Shiina
219	26	🚌 Muroto Aquarium 🚌 Shiina
220	27	
221	28	
222	29	🚌 Muroto Geopark
223	30	🚌 Mitsu 1 Bus Stop, 🛏 Sky and Sea Guesthouse

Day 11: T24, T25, T26 and Cape Muroto	
Distance	21 km
KM	KM 223 – KM 244
🛏	Several places in Kiragawa, Henro House Himitsukichi

After the loneliness of day 10, we have reached an interesting location at the first cape, take enough time to discover the sightseeing spots at Cape Muroto. Our stage is flat except two steep but short climbs to T24 and T26

KM	Daily km	Point of Interest
223	0	🚌 Mitsu 1 Bus Stop, Sky and Sea Guesthouse
224	1	
225	2	🚻
226	3	
227	4	Deep Sea World 🍴, aquatic center 🚻 🛏 El Flamenquito, Raiei-ji (lying buddha)
228	5	🚌 Muroto-Misaki, Mikurodo cave ↗↗ Path uphill, O24 Kannon-Kutsu
229	6	**T24 Hotsumisaki-ji** △ (164 m) ↘↘ Panoramic road downhill, Highway 203
230	7	
231	8	🚌 ⛩ Ojigu 🚻
232	9	🚌 Muroto-Eigyosho hut 🚻 🍴
233	10	
234	11	
235	12	🚌 Muroto Town ♨ **T25 Shinsho-ji**
238	13	
237	14	
238	15	🚻 hut ↗↗ Path to T26
239	16	**T26 Kongocho-ji** △ (140 m)
240	17	↘↘ O26 Fudo-Iwa, 🚌 Shimura Fudo, Highway 55
241	18	
242	19	🚌 🍴 Kiramesse, Whale Museum
243	20	🍴 Sadamaru Burger, Monet's Garden
244	21	🚌 Kiragawa Bridge (Higashi no gawa Eastern River)

Day 12: From Kiragawa to Nahari	
Distance	17 km
KM	KM 244 to KM 261
🛏	In Nahari
	Henro-House Misono

We can sleep longer and be lazy. This is a shorter stage, simply because the last days have been tough, and the first of a series of days along Tosa Bay which is the south coast of Shikoku.

Again, there will be no temple (They are less densely distributed in Kochi Prefecture) but we can include some time to explore the old streets of Kiragawa before we go, and/or Monet's Garden in Nahari if we arrive early.

The walk itself should not take more than 5 hours.

KM	Daily km	Point of Interest
244	0	Kiragawa, antique street
245	1	Bridge over Nishino River (Western River), Hut
246	2	Hut 🚹
247	3	
248	4	⛩
249	5	🍽 Drive-In Ohara, bridge
250	6	🛒
251	7	
252	8	
253	9	🚹
254	10	Goreiseki-Temple 🍽
255	11	🛏
256	12	🚹 Hut 🍽
257	13	Bridge
258	14	Hotel Nahari hot spring ⛩
259	15	🍽🚌🚆 Nahari Station, beginning of railroad to Kochi
260	16	Nahari

Day 13: From Nahari to Aki including T27

Distance	20 km
KM	KM 261 to KM 281
🛏	Henro House Mikeneko, Several options in Aki

Our second stage along Tosa Bay is basically flat and not too long, but for a good reason: The detour from Highway 55 up to T27 and back is a nasty one which includes a Henro-Korogashi (very steep) part. The temple, situated 424 m altitude, is one of the major highlights of the pilgrimage.

KM	Daily km	Point of Interest
261	0	Nahari ⛩
262	1	🚻
263	2	Bridge 🚻 ⛩ Hachimangu
264	3	🚻, leave Route 55, head to the right towards the mountains
265	4	↗↗ (🚉 Tonohama Station 400 m away) Cross railroad
266	5	↗↗ Henro Korogashi ⛩
267	6	**T27 Konomine-ji** △ (424 m)
268	7	↘↘
269	8	↘↘ Hut
270	9	↘↘
271	10	🚉 Tonohama 🛒
272	11	🚌 Yorimichi rest station 🍴 🚻
273	12	🚌
274	13	🚉 Shimoyama
275	14	Cape Oyama 🍴 🚻 Parking 🚌
276	15	🚌⛩ Kamakura Shrine
277	16	🚌
278	17	🚌
279	18	🚻, 🛒, 🚉 Ioki, 🛏 Henro House Mikeneko
280	19	Aki river
281	20	🚉 Aki

Day 14: From Aki to T28 - Approaching Kochi

Distance	25 km
KM	KM 281 to KM 306
🛏	In Konan/Noichi, several options near T28, or in Kochi

Our third day along Tosa Bay takes us to T28, east of Kochi. Traffic gets heavier as we are slowly approaching the next big city.

We are lucky to walk 15 km of our stage on the cycling road which is usually pretty empty and keeps us away from the noisy traffic on highway 55. We can stay in Kochi and return by train to Noichi Station to continue the next day, walking several days without our backpack. By now, we have completed the first quarter of the pilgrimage.

KM	Daily km	Point of Interest
281	0	🚉 Aki 🚻🛒
282	1	🚉 Kyujo-mae, beg. of cycling road 🚻 hut
283-284	2-3	🍴
285	4	⛩ 🚉 Ananai
286	5	
287	6	🚌 Yanagarezan Gokurakuji temple
288	7	Hut 🚻
289	8	🚉 Akano
290	9	
291	10	🚉 Wajiki
292	11	🛒 🚻
293	12	🚉 Nishibun, hut
294	13	Huts, 🚻🛒
295	14	
296	15	Cape Tei Misaki 🚻🛏
297	16	🚉 Yasu, end of cycling road, 🛒🚻🍴
298	17	🛒 ⛩ Kishimoto
299	18	🚉 Kagami 🍴
300	19	🚉 Akaoka
301	20	🛒
302	21	🍴
303	22	🛒, 🍴 Udon, turn right, follow the river
304	23	🚉 Noichi 🛒
305	24	🚌 🛒 Hut
306	25	**T28 Dainichi-ji**

29

Day 15: T29 and T30 - Entering Kochi

Distance	21 km
KM	KM 306 to KM 327 (Kochi Center)
🛏	Near T30

Today's flat stage covers two temples near Kochi and it is calculated until Monjudori Station on the Kochi Tramway which is in the center of Kochi near T31. If we decide to stay in the same place in Kochi for several nights, we can commute from our guesthouse to our stages by public transportation and walk without our backpacks for a change.

In case we have already passed the night in the center of Kochi, we can return to Noichi Station (KM 304), 1.5 km south of T28.

KM	Daily km	Point of Interest
306	0	**T28 Dainichiji,** O28 Tsumebori Yakushido 🍴
307	1	🍴 Coffee shop
308	2	Toitajima bridge over Monobe river
309	3	
310	4	
311	5	Daishido, Henro-goya hut no. 28 🛈
312	6	Railroad crossing
313	7	
314	8	🛒
315	9	Bridge over Kokubu river, 🚌 turn left at the bus stop **T29 Kokubun-ji,** 🍴 Log-Café Cotton-Time
316	10	Bridge
317	11	
318	12	Café Poem, 🛒
319	13	Bridge, detour to O29 Bishamondo waterfalls
320	14	Pass under Kochi Expressway
321	15	Osaka Pass △ (60 m)
322	16	**T30 Zenraku-ji,** O30 ⛩ Tosa-Jinja
323	17	🚉 Tosa-Ikku (train to Kochi) 🛒
324	18	Shimonose bridge over Kokubu river
325	19	🚌
326	20	🛒
327	21	🚉 Monjudori tram to Kochi center

Day 16: T31 - T32 - T33 - Leaving Kochi

Distance	15 km, mostly flat but short steep climbs to T31 and T32
KM	KM 327 to KM 342
⇌	Kochi-ya, near T33, several places near Katsurahama or in Kochi

There will be three temples on our agenda today. The first one, T31, has a splendid area and is situated in Kochi on the top of Godaisan, embedded in a beautiful botanical garden. From this one we will head down the mountain to the sea, visiting T23 situated on a hill overlooking the entire Tosa Bay. We will continue along the seaside farmlands and passing Kochi port before taking the ferry or passing the bridge across the bay.

This is shorter stage, allowing enough time to visit other places on the way, like the botanical garden, having lunch at Katsuo Bune or including a small detour to Katsurahama, the city beach.

We can stay another night in Kochi and continue tomorrow from where we finished. Nagahama bus stop near T33 would be the perfect place to directly return to the center of Kochi (Harimaya Bashi) by bus for the night.

KM	Daily km	Point of Interest
327	0	🚊 Monjudori Tram
328	1	↗↗ **T31 Chikurinji** △ 105m
329	2	↘↘ 🛏
330	3	Henro Bridge over Shimoda River
331	4	Turn right, follow road 247 for 1 km 🍴
332	5	⛩ Karimatsu, turn left across the tunnel
333	6	🚌 Midorigaoka 3-Chome, lake
334	7	↗↗ **T32 Zenjibu-ji** △ 67m↘↘
335	8	Follow Route 14
336	9	⛩ Sumiyoshi (one block south)
337	10	Hut (one block south)
338	11	🛏 (one block south)
339	12	Hut 🍴 Katsuo Bune (one block south) 🛒
340	13	O33 Goza Daishi, ferry (free of charge) 🛏
341	14	Hut 🛏
342	15	**T33 Sekkei-ji** 🛒 🚌 Nagahama ⇌ Kochin-ya

Day 17: T34 and T35 - Across the Flatlands

Distance	27 km
KM	KM 342 to KM 369
🛏	Hostel Utage in Usa, John Mung, Lilian, Shiokaze

We will leave Kochi across the flatlands to T34 in Tosa town and to T35, until we return to the sea near Yokonami Peninsula. At the end of the day, we will be near T36 at the tip of the peninsula, but we will visit T36 tomorrow as it might be too late. Usa is a port town. From far, we will see the bridge to T36 which we will pass tomorrow.

KM	Daily km	Point of Interest
342	0	**T33 Sekkei-ji**
343	1	
344	2	🚻
345	3	
346	4	Bridge over Shinkawa river
347	5	
348	6	
349	7	**T34 Tanema-ji** 🚻
350	8	🍽 Haruno Chaya
351	9	🍽 Ui bakery
352	10	🚻
353	11	Bridge over Niyodo River, 🚻
354	12	Entering Tosa town, 🍽 Udon Self restaurant
355=362	13	🚻 🛒 🍽 McDonald's 🍽 Iwago bakery
356=361	14	🛒 ⛩ 🍽 Mos Burger, Hut 🚻
357	15	
358	16	
359	17	↗↗ **T35 Kyotaki-ji** △ 135m↘↘
360	18	
361	19	🍽 Mos Burger
362	20	🚻, 🛒 🍽 McDonald's 🍽 Iwago bakery
363	21	⛩ Takaishi, bridge over Hage river
364-365	22-23	
366	24	↗△ 30 m↘ Hut 🚻 Decide between tunnel or mountain path
367	25	Mountain path:↗↗△ 202 m↘↘
368	26	Tsunami monument 🛒
369	27	🛒 X Route 23, coast, Usa

Day 18: T36 to T37 Part 1 - Usa to Susaki	
Distance	28 km
KM	KM 368 to KM 396 (Central Susaki)
🛏	Central Susaki

Today our stage takes us from Usa across, or along Yokonami peninsula to the port city of Susaki. We will have another longer stretch to walk, but it is far more entertaining and beautiful and without any major climbs except at the beginning of option 3, if this is our choice.

First, we will visit T36 which is a 5 km walk from Usa over the big bridge to the peninsula. After that, there are several options to continue to Susaki:
1. Taking the common route: From T36 walk back over the bridge as you came, turn left (5km), follow the bay along its northern coast which is another 24 km to Susaki (described in the table).
2. Shortcutting by ferry from Umetate (KM 377 near the big bridge) to Uranouchi (KM 387) which is on the official route This reduces the walking part by 10 km. Plan ahead, as there are only 3 ferries per day, the first one around 7:00 am. Taking the ferry shortens the walking part by 11 km. The most convenient ferry to take is from Umetate at 10:55, but this only works if you leave T36 before 09:45 am.
3. Walking the alternate panoramic route continuing from T36 on the peninsula, almost same distance as official route, 7% climb on the first 2 km, no shops or restaurants until KM 387

Susaki is a port city with wharfs and heavy industry, with several places to spend the night. It can also be reached from Kochi by Railroad.

Usa – T36 - Susaki

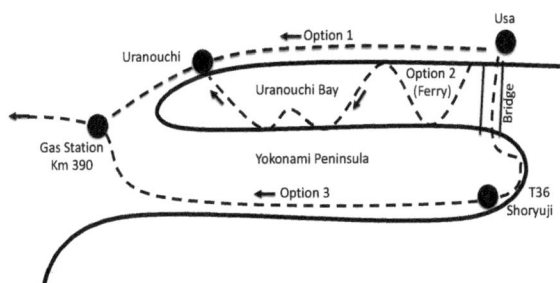

KM	Daily km	Point of Interest
368	0	Usa (Center)
369	1	Usa Marina
370	2	Bridge ramp 🚻
371	3	Bridge end
372	4	🛏 Sanyoso hot springs hotel
373	5	**T36 Shoryuji** beginning of alternate panoramic route on Yokonami Peninsula (no food available, few vending machines)
374	6	
375	7	Ijiri-Daishido
376	8	Bridge (return) 🚻
377	9	Umetate ferry pier 🚻
378	10	🚻
379	11	
380	12	
381	13	Fukaura ferry pier
382	14	
383	15	Bridge
384	16	↗ △ 56 m ↘
385	17	Uranouchi tunnel
386	18	
387	19	Uranouchi ferry pier, 🛒
388	20	
389	21	🚻
390	22	Alternate route meets main route, gas station
391	23	Tosaka tunnel
392	24	Henro-goya hut No. 17 🚻
393	25	
394	26	⛩ Kibune shrine 🛒 cross the river
395	27	Cement plant, bridge
396	28	
396	29	🛏 Susaki, Onogo or Oma 🚻

Day 19: T36 to T37 Part 2 - from Susaki to Tosa-Kure

Distance	14 km
KM	KM 396 to KM 410
🛏	Several options in Tosa Kure

After two longer walking days, today we will afford a "half stage" of only 3 to 4 hours walking including a visit to B5. We can take the time to sleep long, have a late breakfast and visit B5 Daizen-ji overlooking Susaki Bay before continuing to Tosa Kure.

There is a short but challenging stretch after 9 km which is difficult to manage during rain, it can be avoided by following Route 56 from Awa Station, taking the tunnel instead of the pass. Attach a red light to your backpack for better visibility.

KM	Daily km	Point of Interest
396	0	Central Susaki, 🚂 Oma
397	1	🛒
398	2	**B5 Daizen-ji** 🚂 Tosa-Shinjo
399	3	Bridge over Shinjo river, 🍴 🍴
400	4	
401	5	
402	6	
403	7	🚂 Awa, 🛒 (Follow Route 56 across the tunnel for 2.5 km to avoid Yakezaka-Pass)
404	8	(50 m) pass under the railroad ↗↗
405	9	Yakezaka-Pass △ (205 m) ↘↘
406	10	↘ Difficult part avoiding the tunnel
407	11	Hut
408	12	(20 m) Hut 🚌
409	13	
410	14	🚂 Tosa-Kure, 🛒

Day 20: T36 to T37 Part 3 - from Tosa-Kure to T37	
Distance	20 km
KM	KM 410 to KM 430
🛏	Guesthouse of T37, several options in Kubokawa

T37 is too far from Susaki to reach it in one day, that is why we stopped in Tosa-Kure yesterday after a moderate distance. Today we will cover the remaining 20,5 km, mostly along Route 56 which has plenty of traffic. That stage, Route A in the guidebook, is called Soemimizu Henro Trail, it is not too interesting and it includes a tough climb in the beginning.

A way to avoid the tough climb in the beginning is to follow Route B ("Osaka Henro Trail") right from the start along Osaka-dani river, the other river from Tosa-Kure, until reaching Nanako-Pass at Km 6 which spares us a 100 m of altitude. This route is called Soemimizu, it is only 700 m longer.

If you are into some adventure, follow the coastal road from Tosa-Kure, take the detour along Route 25 and 325 (or maybe even 326), which is 6 km (or 10 km) longer but more spectacular. As you will be walking on empty coast and mountain roads. In any case there will be a climb of 300 m in the second half as T37 is located on a plain at higher level, several km away from the coast.

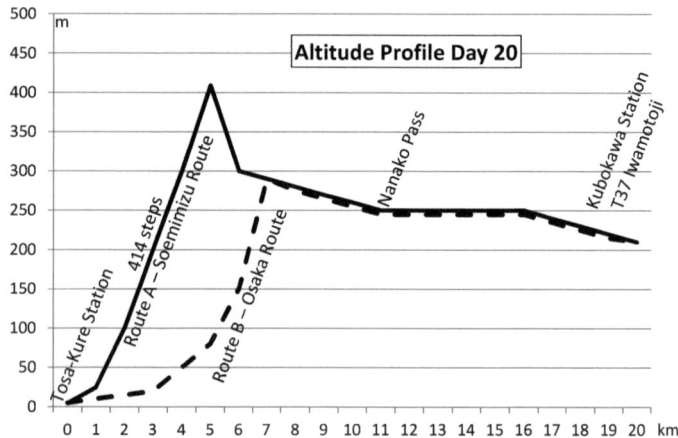

KM	Daily km	Point of Interest
410	0	🚉 🚌 Tosa-Kure (bus available to Nanako pass KM 416) ↗ Choose between Route A along Nagasawa River or Route B along Osaka-dani River to avoid 100 m climb at Km 415
411	1	↗ (25 m)
412	2	↗ Henro-goya hut no. 32, 414 steps
413	3	↗ (200m)
414	4	↗↗ (300m)
415	5	↗↗ △ (409m) highest point
416	6	↘↘ (300m) 🚌 🏢 Nanako-pass (bus from Tosa-Kure) Route A and B join again
417	7	↘ 🍴 Tontaro Nanako Ramen
418	8	
419	9	🚌 🍴 Nakamuraya Udon
420	10	Hut, 🍴
421	11	🚉 Kageno ⛩ Kompira-gu
422	12	🚌 Crossing the railroad
423	13	🚉 Rokutanji 🚌 ⛩ Warei-jinja
424	14	🛒 🍴 Coffee shop
425	15	🚌 🚉 Niida, hut ⛩ 🛏 Guesthouse 40010
426	16	🚌 🍴 🛒
427	17	🚌 🍴 ⛩
428	18	🛒
429	19	Tunnels, 🚉 Kubokawa, 🍴
430	20	**T37 Iwamoto-ji**

Kubokawa is a nice town to stay and even to take a rest for a day.

Takaoka-Jinja, a shrine located 2.5 km east of the town, is the original location of T37. There are 8 or 9 other shrines nearby, which used to belong to T37. The approach over the bridge is the former Sando, the official front approach extending right into the shrine.

Day 21: T37 to T38 Part 1 – From Kubokawa to Cape Ino

Distance	28 km (Challenge)
KM	KM 430 to KM 458
🛏	Several guesthouses near Cape Ino-Misaki

Cape Ashizuri and T38 are still 83 km from T37. We need to walk for four days until we get there, but the walk and the landscape are less monotonous and solitary than the walk to Cape Muroto ten days ago.

We have to cover 28 km today, walking entirely along Route 56. We are crossing an area with no guesthouses, but we have the railway beside us after 11 km from KM 441 and the bus all along Route 56 so we can cut it short if necessary.

After passing Iyoki station, we have can either continue on Route 56 or take an exciting route on tiny roads and passing a small old tunnel at KM 447 and 448, more or less following the railway path. It is beautiful but also easy to get lost on the small village roads.

After 20 km walking across the hills with no major climbs, we will finally reach the coast again and spend our first night either in one of the guesthouses near Cape Inomisaki or on the camping ground 2 km further.

Inside Henro-goya hut no. 13 in Saga, KM 441. Not for sleeping.

38

KM	Daily km	Point of Interest
430	0	T37, Kubokawa (210 m)
431	1	🛒
432	2	⛩ Kinjono-shrine
433	3	🚌 ↗
434	4	↗△ (290m) ↘
435	5	🚌 Daishido turn left, 🍴 Minenoue Yakiniku, shortcut avoiding 2 curves
436	6	↘↘ Hut ℹ️ end of shortcut
437	7	
438	8	🚌
439	9	Hut
440	10	🍴 Shioripan Bakery 🚌 Saga, hut
441	11	Hut
442	12	Henro-goya hut No. 13 🚃 Kaina
443	13	🚌
444	14	⛩Monjudo ⛩ Suga-shrine 🚌
445	15	🚌
446	16	🚌
447	17	🚌 🚃 Iyoki ⛩ Stay on Route 56, or detour
448	18	Detour Kumai tunnel (optional, easy to get lost)
449	19	
450	20	🛒 🍴Yakitori
451	21	🚃 Tosa-Saga hut, 🚌 🍴 Yokohama tunnel
452	22	End of tunnel 🍴
453	23	🚃 Saga-Koen, hut 🚌 ℹ️, seaside
454	24	🚃 Tosa-Shirahama, 🚌 🍴 🛏⛩ Shirao shrine
455	25	Observation deck
456	26	🚌 Nada port, hut, ℹ️ Cape Ino
457	27	Inomisaki tunnel
458	28	🚃 Ariigawa 🚌

Day 22: T37 to T38 Part 2 - Cape Ino to Nakamura	
Distance	16 km
KM	KM 458 to KM 473
🛏	Several guesthouses in Nakamura

After the 30 km of the day before, we can afford a short stage and give our feet a half day rest. Nakamura has a good choice of guesthouses, restaurants and a hot spring. There is also a Montbell sports store.

After this stage, we still have over 42 km walking until we get to Cape Ashizuri, perfect for 2 days.

The pine coast near KM 464 is a good place for outdoor sleeping, camping is quite common in this location.

KM	Daily km	Point of Interest
458	0	🚏 Ariigawa 🚌
459	1	🚏 Tosa-Kamigawaguchi, 🚻
460	2	🚏 Umi-no-Omukae 🏕
461	3	
462	4	🚏 Ukibuchi 🚌
463	5	🏕
464	6	pine coast 🚻,
465	7	🚏 Tosa-Irino, park, 🚻, pine coast
466	8	🚻 🍽 Irinoya Udon 🚌
467	9	🚌
468	10	🚏 Nishi-Ogata 🚌
469	11	🚌
470	12	
471	13	🍽 Joyfull
472	14	
473	15	🚏 Kotsuka, hot spring, 🍽 Mc Donald's
	16	🚏 Nakamura 🛒

Day 23: T37 to T38 Part 3 - From Nakamura to Okinohama

Distance	22 km
KM	KM 473 to KM 495
🛏	Several hotels near Okinohama (KM 494 - KM 496)

From Nakamura we continue along Shimanto river on the east side, the river on our right. After 3 km, we turn left and simply follow Route 321 until our destination which is Okinohama. At KM 483 we have the choice between Shin-izuta tunnel (1.6 km, put your red light on), or the trail over the mountain with an extra 200 m climb. The convenience store at Shimonokae-bridge, KM 490, is the last food store for the next 35 km, but in case we run out of food, we can shortcut to Tosa-Shimizu 3 km from Km 500, 8 km from Okinohama.

KM	Daily km	Point of Interest
473	0	🚃 Kotsuka
474	1	🚌 Kirinuki Bridge
475	2	🚌 Zaisho
476	3	🚃, Shimanto
	4	River Bridge
477	5	Turn left after the bridge, 🚌 Sanzaki, bridge
478	6	⛩ Tenman-gu 🚌
479	7	🚌 Hatsukari, Wild Bird Park,
480	8	Henro-goya hut No. 54, 🍜 Udon, café, 🛈
481	9	Ubi's Road Rest Rest Area (hut)
482	10	🚌 Izuta-Kitazaka
483	11	↗ △(58 m) Tunnel (1.6 km) Imadaishi Temple
484	12	↘ Tunnel
485	13	🚌 Ichinose 🍜 Café 🛈 Shinnen-an Temple
486 - 487	14-15	
488	16	🚌 Ichinono 🍜 Takoyaki
489	17	🚌 Shimonokae Elementary School, bridge
490	18	🚌 Shimonokae-Ogata, bridge
491	19	🛒
492	20	
493	21	🛏 Minshuku Isaribi
494	22	🚌 Kumomo, 🛏 Minshuku Kumomo, 🚌
495	23	🚌 Ikenotani 🚌 Kohama, 🛏 Minshuku Okinohama

Day 24: T37 to T38 Part 4 – The Cape, at Last!

Distance	20 km
KM	KM 495 to KM 515
🛏	Several hotels on Cape Ashizuri

Another highlight: We will finally reach the southernmost point and the most remote of the 88 temples. There is plenty to see around the cape, so take your time. It is 19 to 20 km to the Cape and T38, no matter if we go down the east or the west coast. The sun will shine on the east coast in the morning and from the west in the afternoon, so depending on whether we want sun or shade, we can make our choice. The table describes the east side (Route A) after KM 500:

KM	Daily km	Point of Interest
495	0	🚌 Kohama, 🛏 Minshuku Okinohama
496	1	
497	2	Okinohama Beach 🛈
498	3	🚌 Okinohama Beach
499	4	🚌 Banyo, follow the coast
500	5	🚌 Iburi, beginning of peninsular round trip
		3 km shortcut to Tosa-Shimizu (KM 525, food)
501	6	
502	7	
503	8	Kubotsu village 🚌
504	9	hut 🛈
505	10	🚌 Tsuro village 🛈
506	11	
507	12	🚌 hut
508	13	
509	14	🚌 Tsuro camping 🏕
510	15	🚌 Shishigakoi 🛏
511	16	🚌
512	17	🚌 Ashizuri Higashiguchi 🍴 Kamado
513	18	**T38 Kongofuku-ji**, 🚌 Ashizuri-misaki 🛈
514	19	Scenic spots, Hole into Hell, cape, lighthouse, 🔭
515	20	Landmarks and guesthouses on Cape Ashizuri 🛈

You could also stay at Minshuku Okinohama for two consecutive nights and visit Cape Ashizuri as a 33 km day-trip if you want to save time. But there is so much to see and it is nicer to spend a night at the cape.

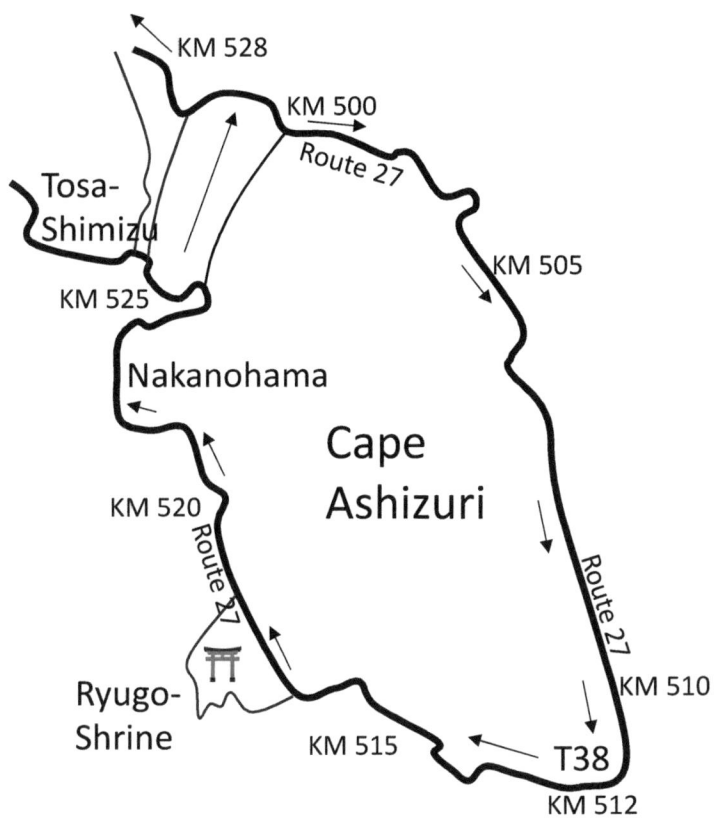

When passing Nakanohama, be aware that it is the birthplace of John "Mung" Manjiro. Take a look at his biography on Wikipedia before visiting his house at KM 521. His life was most amazing. There is also a little Museum in Tosa Shimizu, 3 km from KM 525.

Day 25: T38 to T39 Part 1 - Back to Okinohama

Distance	20 km
KM	KM 514 to KM 534
🛏	Several hotels near Okinohama
	Minshuku Okinohama

We will continue along the coast and over the hill until we close the loop at KM 528 = KM 500 and return to Okinohama for the night. As we are walking back the way we came, there are 10 km in common: KM 490 to 500 are passed again in the other direction becoming KM 529 to KM 539

We can spend the night of day 23 and day 25 in the same location. Tosa-Shimizu will be the last place to shop food for the next 30 km, until we pass Mihara Village two days later.

KM	Daily km	Point of Interest
514	0	Several landmarks on Cape Ashizuri: Hakusan natural arch, footbath, ⛩ Shirayama
515	1	Henro-goya hut No. 20
516	2	⛩ Ishizuchi-jinja
517	3	Hut, panoramic spot
518	4	Matsuo Tunnel (1057 m) or over the hill (100 m climb)
519	5	🚌
520	6	
521	7	🚌 Nakanohama, coffee shop, John Manjiro's birthplace ℹ
522	8	ℹ
523	9	
524	10	
525	11	🚌 Tosa-Shimizu 🚊 🍴 Kashima Park Cross the peninsula to the northeastern coast
526 - 528	12 – 14	
529=500	15	🚌 Iburi, end of peninsula round trip, 9 km back until former KM 490= now KM 538
530=499	16	🚌 Okinohama Beach
531=498	17	🚌 Okinohama Beach
532=497	18	🚌 Okinohama Beach
533=496	19	
534=495	20	🚌 Kohama 🛏 Minshuku Okinohama

Day 26: T38 to T39 Part 2 – Forests and Rivers

Distance	13 km
KM	From KM 534 onwards for 13 km on Route B
🛏	Henro House River Mountain Retreat
	or in Mihara Village, 8 km further (on Route A KM 553)

Our next city is Sukumo, but it is 41 km away. We will spend a night on the way, in the hills of Mihara, an area with limited infrastructure. Today we can sleep longer and be lazy as we just a half day's walk on quiet country roads across hills and forests. (Tomorrow's hike will be longer again, 28 km).

The first 5 km will be back the way we came three days ago. 4 km after our departure we will leave the coast and follow the river upstream at the bridge. There are several routes from T38 to T39. To get to our place to stay, we will follow the route called "Route B" in the Shikoku Japan 88 Route Guide.

Route A is pretty similar in distance and climbs, across a different part of the area. Both routes meet in Mihara at KM 554.

Once we are past the bridge (which we do not cross unless we want to visit the convenience store or the café), the last 9 km are a beautiful, quiet walk along the river across forest and mountains.

Today's stage is calculated to a guesthouse on the countryside called River Mountain Retreat, run by an Australian lady, but you can continue to Mihara Village, 8 km more and shorten tomorrow's stage, as there are other places to stay in the area. Make sure to carry enough food when you are past the convenience store at KM 537, the next shop comes at KM 561.

KM	Daily km	Point of Interest
534/495	0	🚌 Kohama Minshuku Okinohama
535/494	1	🚌
536/493	2	
537/492	3	🏪 (east side of Shimonokae river)
538/491	4	🚌 For Route B follow Route 21 on the same side of the river, do not cross the bridge
539/490	5	🚌 Bridge, beginning of Route B, ☕ Café Poroporo (east side of the river)
Route B	6-12	Follow Route 21 to the west along Shimonokae river
Route B	13	🛏 Henro-House River Mountain Retreat

45

Day 27: T38 to T39 Part 3 - T39 and Sukumo

Distance	27 km
KM	Begin on Route B until KM 574
🛏	Sukumo

Today we have a long, beautiful walk, taking us further across the hills around Mihara along Route 21 without any major climbs. At Km 560 we will pass Umenoki Park and a dam. 5 km later we will find ourselves out of the mountains passing the railroad and approaching T39. After visiting the temple, we have another 7 km to walk until we reach Sukumo.

This is a longer stage, there is an occasional afternoon bus from Mihara Village to Hirata Station.

KM	Daily km	Point of Interest
Alternate Route	0	🛏 Henro-House River Mountain Retreat
	1-4	🔺
	5	⛩ Tenmangu 🈁 Hosen-ji temple
553-555	6-8	Mihara Village, turn left, Miyanokawa tunnel,
556	9	🚌 turn right follow Route 21
557	10	
558-559	11	Umenoki Park 🈁 hut
560	13	Dam, hut 🈁
561	14	↘ 🚌 Kurokawa wildlife park
562	15	↘
563	16	↘ X Route 21/Route 56, turn left, follow Route 56 🚌 Hirata Stn., 🍜, 🈁
564	17	🚌 Terao, 🚌 Terayamaguchi turn right, leave Route 56 for T39
565	18	
566	19	**T39 Enko-ji**, O39
567	20	Return to Route 56, turn right 🚌 🍽
568	21	🚌 (Half distance of the entire pilgrimage)
569	22	🚌 Komori,
570	23	🚌 Asahi-Shokuhin-Mae, 🍜, 🍽 Tsurukame
571	24	
572	25	🈁 Henro-goya hut no. 33, 🚉 Higashi-Sukumo
573	26	Sukumo
574	27	🚉 🚌 Sukumo

Day 28: Half-Time at T40

Distance	20 km
KM	KM 574 to KM 594
⏤	Near T40 or guesthouse of T40 in Ainan

It is time to celebrate. Today we will enter the third of Shikoku's four prefectures. Also, we are beginning the second half of the pilgrimage distance, half the pilgrimage was completed at KM 568.5, after leaving T39 yesterday.

We will leave Sukumo over the mountain range to the north and follow Shikoku's wild and spectacular east coast from there. There is a climb of up to 300 m with 7 km of forest trail, which can be avoided by following Route 56 and passing a tunnel. The rest is a fairly easy hike.

KM	Daily km	Point of Interest
574	0	🚌 Sukumo 🍴 Pilgrimage route leaves the road to the left, bridge, ⛩ Itsukushima shrine
575	1	
576	2	
577	3	↗↗
578	4	↗↗
579	5	↗↗ Pass △ (300 m), Matsuo Daishi ruins, hut 🛈
580	6	
581	7	↘↘
582	8	↘
583	9	Matsuo daishi
584	10	X Route 56 🍴 🚌 Follow Route B in the Route Guide, Route A along Route 56 is 800 m shorter but monotonous and does not pass toilets and shops.
585	11	Kotaku daishido
586	12	
587	13	(100 m)
588	14	🚌 🛈, ⛩ Omiya, hut
589	15	
590	16	🛈 hut
591	17	🚌 🍴 Turn left, follow the river, Butsugari-In
592	18	Bridge ⛰ uphill
593	19	**T40 Kanjizai-ji**, 🍴 Ainan, 🚌 Hirajo-fudasho-mae
594	20	Ainan 🍴 🍱

Day 29: Along the West Coast

Distance	24 km
KM	KM 594 to KM 619
🛏	Several options in Tsushima

We have left Kochi, the prefecture with the lowest "temple concentration", but we will still walk 50 km (2 days) until reaching T41. Time to enjoy the panorama of the rock coast and its many rocks and tiny islands during our walk to Tsushima along Route 56.

From KM 604, we can also follow Route 56 along the coast, it is easier to walk and has huts, camping, toilets, restaurants and a beautiful view but it is 2 km longer.

KM	Daily km	Point of Interest
594	0	🚃 Ainan
595	1	🚃 🛒 🍽 Udon, Joyfull
596	2	🚃
597 - 598	3 - 4	
599	5	🚃 ⛩ Itsukushima
600	6	🚃 Kikugawa-shogakko-mae
601	7	🚃
602	8	🚃 Panoramic point to the left, 🛖
603	9	🍽 Café Alpha
604	10	🚃 Hut 🛒 🛖 official route leaves Route 56 across the hills for 9 km. Coastal route is 2 km longer but without climbs.
605	11	↗ Hut
606	12	↗ Yanaginomizu-Daishi Temple, 🛖
607	13	↗ 🏔 on the coastal road (Route 56)
608	14	△ (460 m) Shimizu Daishi Temple
609	15	Hut ↘↘
610 - 613	16 - 19	
614	20	Official route meets Route 56 again, 🚃 Daimon (100 m left)
615	21	🛖 Henro-goya hut no. 19, 🚃 Hataji
616	22	
617	23	🚃 Kamoda, 🍽 Yakimura
618	24	🚃 Kongobashi
619	25	🛒 Tsushima 🛖 🍽 🚃

Day 30: From Tsushima to Uwajima

Distance	15 km
KM	KM 619 to KM 634
⛏	Several options in Uwajima

As Uwajima is a good place to stay, this one is again a shorter stage allowing time to sleep out, give our legs a rest, do some washing and to enjoy the city. And we can have a good lunch somewhere on the way.

We will mostly walk along Route 56, but we can avoid the highway in many places and walk in parallel on quieter country roads.

After 3 km, at KM 622, there will be a tunnel section. We need to decide between 1.1 km of tunnel or an additional 1 km more to walk with 160 m of climb if we go over the hill

Visit B6, Warei-shrine, the castle and Tensha-en Garden. The area near the train station has a good choice of restaurants and a public bath.

KM	Daily km	Point of Interest
619	0	🚌 Tsushima center
620	1	🍴
621	2	🚌 🛒 🍴 bakery, coffee shop
622	3	🍴 Bakery 🚌 Matsuo-tunnel: Decide between Matsuo tunnel (1710 m along Route 56) or mountain path (↗↗ 160 m climb ↘↘)
623-625	4-6	
626	7	🚌 Noi, End of tunnel section Mountain path detour ends on Route 56
627	8	🍴 Café
628	9	🚌 Ishimaru 🛒 🍴 Joyfull
629	10	🚌🛒 🈁
630	11	🍴 🛒
631	12	🚌 Kawachi-guchi 🍴 Sushiro & Komeda's Coffee
632	13	🛒 🍴 O40 Mameki Daishi
633	14	🚌 Uwajima Bus Center, Uwajima castle
634	15	🚆 Uwajima, B6/O40 Ryukoin ⛩ Warei-Jinja

Day 31: T41 - T42 - T43: Three in a Row!

Distance	24 km
KM	KM 634 to KM 658
🛏	Several options in Unomachi

We will visit three temples today. T41 and T42 are on the countryside in a slightly remote area, while T43 is near the city of Unomachi. The walk is mostly flat however it includes a 4 km spart with a steep climb of 300 m altitude in the middle, which can easily be avoided by simply staying on Route 31 and walking 420 m across Hanaga tunnel.

KM	Daily km	Point of Interest
634	0	🚃 Uwajima, B6/O40 Ryuko-in
635	1	🛒 Supermarket 🛒
636	2	🚃 Kita-Uwajima 🎫
637	3	🚌 Nenashigawa
638-639	4-5	🚌 Torigoe 🚌 Barin-guchi 🚌 Nakahata
640	6	🚌 Sinyashiki, Henro-goya hut no. 21
641	7	Jizo-statue
642	8	🚌 🚃Muden, Bridge
643	9	🍢 Mike Takoyaki Restaurant, 🍢 Chomeisui
644	10	**T41 Ryuko-ji**
645	11	🚌 Ishigahana, turn right, continue on Route 31
646	12	
647	13	🚌 **T42 Butsumoku-ji** (184 m) Turn left at the bridge ↗ 1 km of trail
648	14	Back on Route 31, choose between Hanaga tunnel and pass ↗↗ 400 m of trail
649	15	↗↗ hut, trail on the right, Hanaga-Pass △ (495 m)
650	16	↘↘ O42 Miokuri Daishi
651	17	↘↘ (194 m) Hut, Hanaga-jizo, bridge, turn left, 🚌 Hanaga-toge, follow Route 29 along the river
652	18	Michibiki-daishi ⛩
653	19	
654	20	🚌 Mikudani, Inamori-daishi, Hut, 🚃 Shimouwa, leave Route 29 right (210 m)
655	21	
656	22	🛒 turn right ↗ O43 Hakuo-gongen
657	23	**T43 Meiseki-ji** △ (273 m)
658	24	🚃 🚌 Unomachi

Day 32: T43 to T44 Part 1 – Unomachi to Ozu

Distance	22 km
KM	KM 658 to KM 680
🛏	Ozu

The distance between T43 and T44 is 70 km, 3.5 days of walking without passing any of the 88 temples. Ozu is one of Shikoku's best-kept secrets, with some other nice places to visit: A Samurai house (Garyu Sanso) and garden, the castle, a toy museum and an excellent Onsen (Garyu no Yu). The walk is basically flat along Route 59.

KM	Daily km	Point of Interest
658	0	🚍🚌 Unomachi
659	1	🛒🚌 Shimomatsuba 🍴
660	2	🚍🚌 Kami-Uwa 🍴🍴 leave Route 59, walk small road in parallel for 2.4 km
661	3	🚌🍴🏨🍴 hut, stone marker
662-663	4-5	🚌 back on Route 59
664	6	🚌🍴🏨🍴 Coffee House leave Route 59 and walk in parallel for 1.5 km
665	7	🚌 Higashi-tada ⛩ Yasaka-shrine, Taba-ji
666	8	🚌 Shiba 🍴 Coffee shop Bechika House, leave Route 59 to the right for country road for 500 m, stone markers, temple, 🍴 Moss Garden
667	9	🚌 Masanobu 🍴 Henro-goya hut no.49, Ryuko-ji 🍴 Music Cafe
668	10	🚌 Kubo 🏨 hut, alternate route 150 m climb avoiding tunnel, ⛩ Taga-shrine, Tosaka Tunnel (1117 m)
669	11	🚌 end of tunnel (alt. 300 m) ↘ 🚌 Sambonmatsu
670-672	12-14	↘
673	15	↘ 🚌 Ozu Golf Club (alt. 100 m)
674	16	🚌 Kitada, hut, 🏨 (alt. 15 m) Kasamitomi-river
675	17	🚌 Route 59 turns left under Expressway 🍴
676	18	🚌 Tunnel, Juei-ji 🍴🍴 old part of Ozu
677	19	🍴 Joyfull
678	20	Bridge over Hijikawa River, Garyo-no-yu Onsen, ⛺ (2 km east)
679	21	Yoshino-yu Onsen
680	22	🚍🚌 Ozu 🍴

Day 33: T43 to T44 Part 2 – A Famous Bridge

Distance	12 km
KM	KM 680 to KM 692
🛏	Uchiko: Yamamomo or Uchikobare

We will give our legs a rest today by walking just 11-12 km for about three hours, from Ozu to the city of Uchiko. This will allow us to explore Ozu and the old part of Uchiko, and to turn the next two days into bearable distances.

When leaving Ozu, after walking for 3 km straight across a boring industrial and commercial area, we will visit B8 Toyogahashi, a famous Bekkaku temple dedicated to the bridge under which Kobo Daishi once slept, according to legend. Go and have a look, he is still there, sleeping under his blankets.

The temple was destroyed in a flood in 2018 and had to be rebuilt, so be generous with your donation.

KM	Daily km	Point of Interest
680	0	🚉🚌 Ozu 🛒
681	1	🍽 Joyfull
682	2	🛒
683	3	**B8 Toyogahashi**, 🛒 🚻 🍽
684	4	
685	5	🚌 Niiya, 🚻
686	6	🚌 Kitayama, 🛒
687	7	hut
688	8	
689	9	🚌 Ikazaki, 🛒
690	10	↗ △ (118 m) ↘
691	11	🚉 Uchiko 🛒 🚻 🍽
692	12	🚌 Uchiko 🚻 ⛰

Day 34: T43 to T44 Part 3 – Into the Mountains

Distance	22 km
KM	KM 691 to KM 712
🛏	Tado Village

There are no convenience stores and almost no restaurants on the 35 km between Uchiko and Kuma-Kogen, so we need food and drink for two days.

We will follow Route A in the Route Guide. The walk begins smoothly along Oda-River for the first 15 km until KM 706. There are two places to stay in Tado village.

Route B in the Route Guide is easier to walk especially during critical weather as it is all paved until Kuma Kogen.

KM	Daily km	Point of Interest
691	0	🚉 Uchiko 🛒 🏧 🍱 (56 m)
692	1	🍱 Uchiko Fresh Park, Road Station, Farmer's Mkt.
693-694	2-3	
695	4	🛒 Food shop
696	5	
697	6	↗ Hut
698	7	↗
699	8	↗ Hut, 🚌 Kakegi (84 m)
700	9	🚌 Ose Bus Stop
701	10	
702	11	🚌 Otsunaru, Hut
703	12	Hut
704	13	🚌 , Hut
705	14	Bridge
706	15	🚌 Umezu. Turn left, stay on Route 379, pass Yoshinokawa Tunnel 🚌 Tsukiawase, for "Route B", follow the Oda river on Route 380
707	16	End of tunnel, Henro-goya hut No. 38
708	17	↗
709	18	↗ Daishido
710	19	↗🍱 Namihei Udon Nitta Hachiman ⛩, 🏧 (170 m)
711	20	↗ Hut, 🏧
712	21	🛏 Tado Village (200 m)

Day 35: T43 to T44 Part 4 – To Kuma-Kogen

Distance	15 km, including 680 m climb
KM	KM 712 to KM 727
🛏	Kuma-Kogen, several options

Today's walk will be not long but challenging as we will walk over two passes and steeply down into the valley where Kuma-Kogen and T44 are located. The walk involves some trails.

Leave Tado village before 10 am to make sure to reach Kuma-Kogen before sunset as the 4 km across the forest between KM 722 and 726 are difficult to walk in the dark.

KM	Daily km	Point of Interest
712	0	🚹 🛏 Tado Village (200 m)
713	1	↗ Ochiai Tunnel (231 m) After the tunnel, follow Route 379 only for O51 Ishizuchiji, otherwise follow Route 42 to the right at the huts
714	2	↗
715	3	↗
716	4	↗ Daishido
717	5	↗ ⛩ Mishima-jinja, 🚹 (346m)
718	6	↗ Shortcut (signs) to save 1 km: follow the small road to the left
719	7	↗ Daishido (412 m) ↗↗ Shimosakaba Pass △ (570 m)
720	8	Paved road ends. Walk trail for about 300 m
721	9	↘ ⛩ Katsuragi, turn left (527 m), cross Route 220, over the bridge, turn left, across the village, turn right at the wooden signpost (check the map!)
722	10	Morita-daishido. Beginning of forest trail ↗ Hut (600 m)
723	11	↗↗ 🛏 Yuranomori Guest House (700 m)
724	12	↗ Hiwada Pass △ (790 m) hut
725	13	↘ (600 m)
726	14	↘↘ X Route 33 (473 m), continue straight for T44
727	15	Bridge ↗ **T44 Daiho-ji** (550 m)

Day 36: The Loop to T45 and back

Distance	14 km (Challenge)
KM	KM 728 to KM 742
⊨	Several places near Kogen Golf Club

This is another day without restaurants or shops on our way.

We will leave T44 to the east and follow the Henro-michi (pilgrim's trail) along a valley and visit Temple 45, it is at the end of a loop. T45 is an almost vertical mountain temple built into the rocks (reminding of T27). The idea is that we approach T45 from the top (route A), leave T45 at the bottom (Route B). The stage contains plenty of ups and downs, 650 m of climbs, and an extremely steep downhill part just before we arrive at T45.

We can spend the night at one of the places near Kogen Golf Club, there are guesthouses and a campground, or at the same place in Kuma-Kogen where we stayed last night.

KM	Daily km	Point of Interest
728	0	↗ **T44 Daiho-ji** (550 m) follow the Henro trail east, ↗↗ Tonomido Pass △ (730 m)
729	1	↘↘ (606 m)
730	2	↘ 🏨 ⛩ Sumiyoshi (525 m)
731	3	🚌 Hatanogawa, Guesthouses ⚠
732	4	Golf course, leave Route 12 at the hut (560 m)
733	5	Follow the trail on the right at the white signs
734	6	Beginning of loop, turn right for T45 top approach, ↗↗ Hachozaka slope △ (734 m)
735	7	↗
736	8	↗ △ (785 m) ↘↘ O45 Seriwari-Zenjo, 36 Statues
737	9	Very steep ↘↘ **T45 Iwaya-ji** (567 m)
738	10	↘↘ (442 m) 🚌 Iwayaji-mae Furuiwaya Tunnel
739	11	🚌 Kyosebachi bus stop, hut, 🏨, Furuiwaya-so Hotel, panoramic point
740=734	12	Follow the river to the left, Daishido, end of loop
741=733	13	
742=732	14	Guesthouses, golf course ⚠

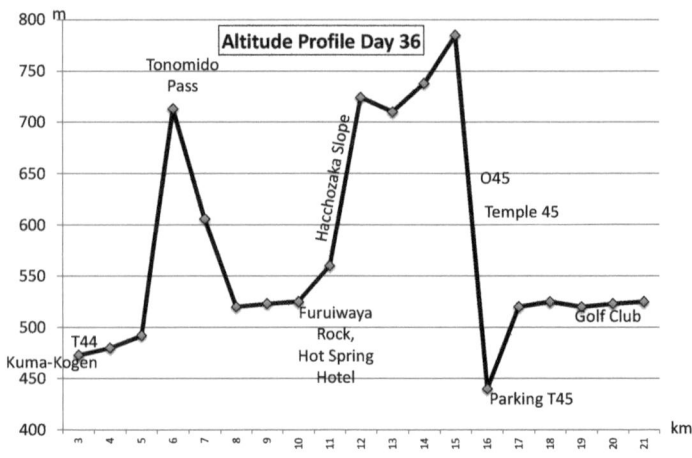

Altitude Profile Day 36

Tonomido Pass

Hacchozaka Slope

O45
Temple 45

Furuiwaya Rock, Hot Spring Hotel

T44
Kuma-Kogen

Golf Club

Parking T45

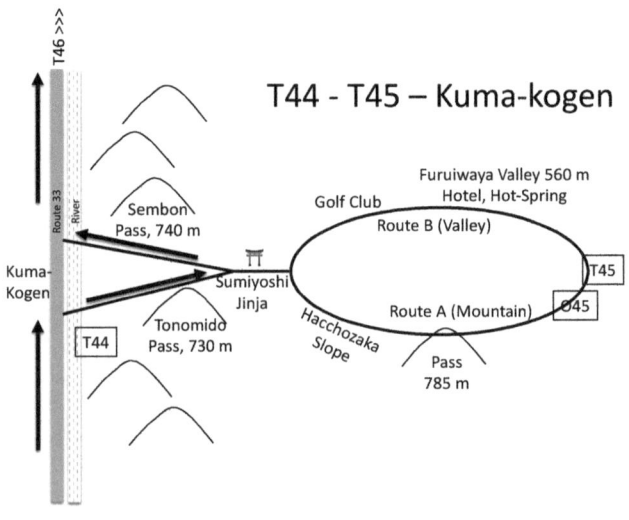

T44 - T45 – Kuma-kogen

T46 >>>

Route 33

River

Sembon Pass, 740 m

Furuiwaya Valley 560 m
Hotel, Hot-Spring

Golf Club

Route B (Valley)

Kuma-Kogen

Sumiyoshi Jinja

T45

O45

T44

Tonomido Pass, 730 m

Hacchozaka Slope

Route A (Mountain)

Pass 785 m

Day 37: Leaving the Mountains to T46

Distance	20 Km
KM	KM 743 to KM 763
🛏	Chochin-ya

After a final climb 7 km after Kuma-Kogen, it's downhill into the plains south of Matsuyama! After that, there will be no major climbs for the next four days.

At the beginning of our walk, Sembon Pass (KM 746) might be overgrown and, as described here, can be avoided by staying on Route 12 across Tonomido Tunnel until reaching Kuma. We will avoid a climb of over 100 m that way. This allows us to grab some food at the stores in Kuma, the next store is 20 km away.

KM	Daily km	Point of Interest
743	0	Guesthouses, ⛰ (525 m) 🚌 Hatanogawa,
744	1	Optional trail over Sembon Toge Pass (right)
-	2	Tonomido Tunnel (700 m long)↗ stay on Route 12
-	3	End of tunnel ↘ 🚌
748	4	🚌 Togoku ↘ hut 🚌 Kuma 🏨 X Route 33, turn right (512 m)
748	5	🏨 🍜 Ramen
749	6	↗ ⛩ Kodono 🏨 (542 m)
750	7	⛩, Place of worship
751	8	↗ Farmer's market, Kayo-chan House (rest place) 🚌 Yokodori (580 m)
752	9	↗ Road traffic turns into tunnel to the left, cars only! (600 m), we continue straight uphill.
753	10	↗ (643 m) 🏨
754	11	↗ Misaka Pass △ (702 m),
755	12	↘ leave Route 440 to the right, take the 2.4 km trail downhill on the right just before the main road takes a left turn. (Several signposts) Sakura Rest Hut
756	13	↘ Rest hut (500 m)
757	14	↘ Sakamotoya (legendary rest hut) 🏨 (318 m)
758	15	↘ End of trail section
759	16	↘ Amikake-ishi temple (177 m)
760	17	↘ 🏨
761	18	↘ (90 m) Go left
762	19	↘ (68 m)

763	20	🚌 **T46 Joruri-ji,** 🛏 Chochin-ya hostel

Day 38: T47 to T51 - Entering Matsuyama

Distance	14 km
KM	KM 763 to KM 777
🛏	Many options Matsuyama

Today's stage is mostly flat, except for occasional temples on hills. On this stage we will experience the change from rural landscape to the bustling city. Despite the short distance, this will be a busy day, as we have six temples on our agenda which includes a visit to B9, and we might even include some shrines or Okunoins. With 30 minutes per temple and one hour for T51, our day will consist of

- 5 hours of walking with shorter breaks
- 1 hour for T51
- 2.5 hours for the 5 other temples
- 1 hour lunch break

We will be on our way for 9 to 10 hours, so despite the shorter distance, we need to be on our way before 8 am if we want to get to T51 before 5 pm.

KM	Daily km	Point of Interest
763	0	🚌 **T46 Joruri-ji,** Chochin-ya hostel
764	1	🚌 **T47 Yasaka-ji**
765	2	⛩ Suwa-shrine, **B9 Monjuin,** grave mounds
766	3	
767	4	Fudahajima Daishido, Inari ⛩, Bridge over Shigenobu River
768	5	🛒
769	6	**T48 Sairinji,** O48 Jonofuchi 🏪 🍴 Okonomiyaki
770	7	🚌 🚌 🚌
771	8	🍴 Ramen 🚌 🍴
772	9	**T49 Jodo-ji,** O49 Ushinomine, 🚌 🚋 Kume. Follow Route 40 for 500 m. At the Chinese take-away on the left follow the narrow road on the right with the white pilgrim signs on the pavement for 100 m. Then walk towards the cemetery.
773	10	↗ **T50 Hanta-ji**
774	11	⛩ Kuwabara Hachiman 🏪
775	12	🏪 Lawsons
776	13	Crossing Ishite River, 🛒 **T51 Ishiteji** (Plan at least one hour)
777	14	Dogo-Onsen, 🚋 tram to Matsuyama

Day 39: T52 and T53 - Leaving Matsuyama

Distance	23 km
KM	KM 777 to KM 800
🛏	Several Options in Hojo

After maybe spending one or two days to rest in Matsuyama, our next walking day will be a mostly flat walk to the two temples north of Matsuyama. We will then continue further along the coast, heading north for another 11 km in the direction of Imabari. This is an easy, panoramic stage but very busy with plenty of traffic. Kashima Island is a tiny island next to the coast.

KM	Daily km	Point of Interest
777	0	Dogo Onsen
778	1	🛒
779	2	Central Matsuyama 🛒
780	3	Turn right on Route 136 🏧 🛒 stone marker
781	4	🛒
782	5	Turn left
783	6	Batto-kanon stone
784	7	Anjo-ji, cross the railroad
785	8	⛩ Taishogun Jinja 🏧 turn right
786	9	🚌 Taisanji, first gate, second gate
787	10	↗ **T52 Taisanji** △ (70 m), 2 km detour to O52 Kyogamori (203 m) panorama↘
788	11	🍽
789	12	🚌 **T53 Enmyo--ji**, 🚆 Iyo-Wake
790	13	🛒 🏧 🛒 🏧
791	14	
792	15	🚆 Horie. 🛒 🏧
793	16	🍽 Café Train
794	17	
795	18	🍽 Kaisen Hokuto 🚆 Koyodai
796	19	Renpukuji 🏧 🚆 Awai
797	20	🚆 Yanagihara
798	21	🍽 🛒 Ninoshita Daishido
799	22	🍽 🛒
800	23	🚆 Iyo-Hojo Kashima-Island ⛰

Day 40: T54 and T55 - To the Northwestern Cape	
Distance	28 km
KM	KM 800 to KM 828
🛏	Several options in Imabari

Today we will head in the direction of the northwestern cape of Shikoku, but just before reaching it, we will use a shortcut over cape to Imabari, a city hosting several temples. On the way, we will visit T54 and T55 before checking into our accommodation in the city. The other four temples near Imabari are left for tomorrow.

The walk is 28 km but flat, and we will be walking along the railway for most of our stage, more or less following Route 196 or the smaller roads running parallel. We have the option to walk over the hills on the first 5 km, the climb is just 72 m and it reduces the distance by 1.4 km

The petrochemical complex at KM 814 is a group of overground and underground liquid natural gas tanks.

All in all, this is a stage with a good infrastructure. But if the 28 km of this stage get too long, we can stop in Imabari after 27 km and visit T55 the next morning, or we can do a part by train.

Looking north at KM 806

Full km	Daily km	Point of Interest
800	0	🚌 Iyo-Hojo, Kashima island ⛰
801	1	🛒. Follow the coast on Route 196 or head north into the hills
802	2	🚌, Kama Daishi
803	3	🚌, Konosaka slope △ (72 m) 🛈 hut
804	4	🚌, Mikuri Amida-do (Place of worship)
805	5	X Route 196 🚌 Asanami 🍴 Bakery, Okonomiyaki 🍴
806	6	
807	7	🍴 🍴 Ko-Shrine (pass the railroad)
808	8	
809	9	🍴 🍴Kompiragu 🍴Ryu
810	10	🚌 Henjo-in Temple 🚌 Kikuma 🛒 🍴 Udon
811	11	🚌🛒
812	12	🛒
813	13	🛒 Aoki Jizo temple, hut, 🍴 Petrochemical complex (underground gas tank)
814	14	🚌🚌, Iyo-Kameoka, 🛈 Enpuku-ji
815	15	🚌 Enfukuji 🛈 🍴 Karaage
816	16	🚌
817	17	🚌🛈 🍴 Udon
818	18	🚌🛈
819	19	🚌🛒
820	20	🚌🚌 Onishi 🍴 Shinko-ji
821	21	🚌🛒
822	22	
823	23	Leave Route 196, continue straight along the canal at 🍴 Kanto Ramen 🚌
824	24	🚌🛒 Turn right at the bus stop 🛈 **T54 Enmei-ji**
825	25	Memorial Park
826	26	🛈
827	27	🛈 🍴 Himesaka 🛒 🚌 Imabari
828	28	**T55 Nankobo**

Day 41: T56 to T59 and to Nyugawa

Distance	28 km
KM	KM 829 to KM 855 + 2 km
🛏	Several options in Saijo, GH Bekku KM 859

We have reached the north coast of Shikoku and the Seto Inland Sea. From far, we can see the bridges connecting Shikoku with Honshu near the city of Imabari. We will follow the coast to the south with a bit of zig-zag into the hills, visiting four temples today. There is a short nasty climb to T58. Nyugawa has several places to stay, it is 2 km from the route off KM 855.

Full km	Daily km	Point of Interest
829	0	🚆 Imabari
830	1	🍴 Kotobukiya Trad.
831	2	**T56 Taisan-ji,** O56 Ryusenji
832	3	🚌 Koizumi, Henro-goya Hut No. 41, turn right at the river, stone marker
833	4	Cross the river 🍴 Nijiiro traditional cooking
834	5	Osugi, hut, **T57 Eifuku-ji** (40 m)
835	6	⛩ Oyamazumi 🚻 reservoir
836	7	↗ (180 m) hut
837	8	↗↗ **T58 Senyuji** △ (280 m)
838	9	↘
839	10	↘⛩ Kichijoji
840	11	🍴 Bakery
841	12	🚻 🚆 Iyo-Tomita (150 m left), turn right
842	13	🍴 Okamin Coffee
843	14	🚌 🚻 **T59 Kokubun-ji**
844	15	🚻
845	16	🚆 Iyo-Sakurai
846	17	🍴 Astro Cafe
847	18	Cycling Road
848	19	Handycraft Museum, Yunoura Onsen
849	20	🚻🏔
850	21	🚻 Okunoin Sendanji
851	22	
852	23	Usui-Goraigo Temple
853	24	Higiri Daishi 🚆 Iyo-Miyoshi (500 m)
854	25	Higiri Daishi 🚻
855	26	2 km to 🚆 Iyo-Nyugawa 🚻

Day 42: A Tough Day - T60 to T62	
Distance	27 km (Challenge)
KM	4 km + KM 859 to KM 882
⊨	Business Hotel Komatsu, ⚠, Nojima House

Challenging! Not many places to spend the night, and the climb to T60 is very steep. I have planned this stage to Iyo-Komatsu Station, but he city of Iyo-Saijo is just 3 train stations away and offers more accommodations. (You can return to Iyo-Komatsu the next morning and continue from here). Another possibility would be to stay at Nojima House, a private accommodation managed by one of the "trail angels" next to T62. T62 is near T61 but it might be already closed when we arrive. Planning T62 and even T61 for the next day will reduce time pressure.

The stage includes two Bekkaku temples, B10 and B11 with minor detours, which are close together. B10 is an impressive mountain temple in a beautiful location but at an altitude of 262 m. Visiting these two temples will add another 5 km to the stage.

The hardest part is at the middle when we have to climb 3 km to T60, facing a "Henro Korogashi" section just before reaching the temple. Today's stage is difficult and remote, take along enough food and drink, and be prepared for colder temperatures in the mountains. This stage might take 10 to 12 hours. Make sure to leave T60 before 5 to reach the paved section after 22 km at KM 877 before sunset.

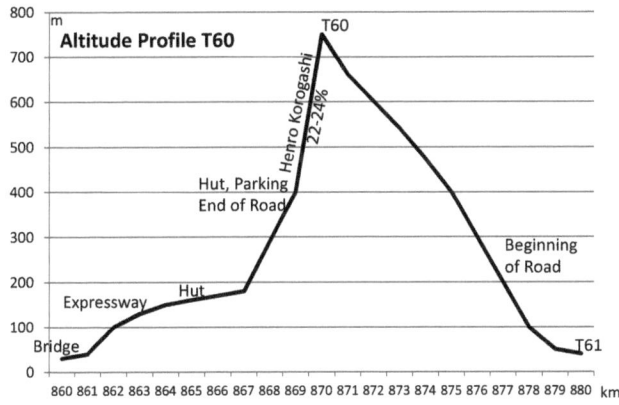

KM	Daily km	Point of Interest
	0	🏯 Iyo-Nyugawa, follow Route 48 straight to the hills
	(856)	⛩ Warei-jinja, detour to **B10**
4	859	X Route 48 to/from Nyugawa, Shozen-ji 🛈 🍴🛏
5	860	X Route 147 at the 🍴, turn left, detour to **B11**
6	861	Bridge over Nakayama river
7	862	🍴 O60 Myounji (This spot is a good place for a final break before the big climb)
8	863	Pass under expressway
9	864	
10	865	Hut, Daishido (100 m)
11	866	↗
12	867	↗ (200 m)
13	868	↗ Hut (272 m) 🛈
14	869	↗↗ Beginning of the hard part, end of paved section
15	870	↗↗ Henro Korogashi (500 m)
16	871	↗↗ **T60 Yokomine-ji** △ (750 m) Option to continue to Mount Ishizuchi from here (11 km/5h)
17	872	↘ 🚌 (Bus connection to 🏯 Iyo-Saijo, KM 892)
18	873	↘↘
19	874	↘
20	875	↘ (474 m) alternate Route to ⛰ site, after 3 km
21	876	↘ Hut (370 m)
22	877	↘ Beginning of paved section
23	878	Hut, O61 Shirataki
24	879	Pass under expressway
25	880	O61 Takagamo-jinja, **T61 Koon-ji**
26	881	O60 Seirakuji 🛈
27	882	🍴 🏯 Iyo-Komatsu, **T62 Hoju-ji,** 🛏 Nojima House

In case you run out of time or energy on this long part, there is a shuttle bus from T60 at the temple parking to another bus stop halfway downhill (Yokomine Tozanguchi) from where you can get to T63 by walking or with another bus. Check the schedule before visiting the temple.

Day 43: Straight and Flat - T62 - T63 - T64

Distance	20 km
KM	KM 882 to KM 903
🛏	Several options in Niihama City, 3 km north of KM 902

This easier stage will take us along Route 11. In case we did not make it yesterday, we can start with visits to T61 and T62. The walk along the highway can be monotonous, but from T63 at KM 883 and again from the Gas Station at KM 893 we can walk smaller roads for several km. We will be passing the city of Iyo-Saijo from where we can include a detour to Mount Ishizuchi (1,982 m), the highest peak of Shikoku. There is a bus connection to the ropeway.

There are not many perfect places to sleep at the end of this stage. BH Misono is in a convenient spot, and there are several hotels in Niihama City, 2 km north (left) of our route.

KM	Daily km	Point of Interest
882	0	🚌 **T62 Hoju-ji**, 🚆 Iyo-Komatsu 🍴
883	1	🚌 🍱 🍴 **T63 Kichijo-ji** 🚆 Iyo-Himi, 🍴
884	2	🚌 Walk parallel to Route 11 for 4 km
885	3	🚌
886	4	🚌 🚆 Ishizuchiyama ⛩ O64 Ishizuchi Jinja **T64 Maegami-ji**
887	5	🚌 ℹ️ 🍴
888	6	🚌
889	7	🚌 Bridge over Kamo-river
890	8	🚌 🍴 🍱 Joyfull
891	9	🚌 🍴 🚆 Iyo-Saijo (500 m north)
892	10	🚌 🍱 Fukutake Shokudo 🍴
893	11	🚌 🍴 ENEOS gas station, follow the smaller road on the right
894	12	🚌 Bridge over Muro River,
895	13	🚌 🍴 Jizodo ⛩
896	14	🚌 🍴 Hut
897	15	🚌
898	16	🚌 🍴
899	17	🚌 🍴 🍱 Joyfull
900	18	🚌 🍴
	19 - 20	🚌 ℹ️ 🍴 🍴 Niihama (1-2 km north)

Day 44: Along the Inland Sea to Iyo-Mishima

Distance	26 km
KM	KM 902 to KM 926
🛏	Several options in Iyo-Mishima

Today the pilgrimage continues from Henro Goya Hut No. 55, one block south of Highway 11 on the old highway named Kyukaido. No major temples today the Seto inland sea. We will pass Bekkaku Temple No. 12. This is a flat, easier hike. But less interesting as we continue straight along Route 11 to Iyo-Mishima.

KM	Daily km	Point of Interest
	1	🚌🚻🛒🛒 Niihama
902	2	Henro-goya hut no. 55 🍴 🚌 300 m
903	3	Bridge over Kokuryo-river 🍴 Udon 🚌 100 m
904	4	🚌⛩🛒 Kyukaido meets Route 11, daishido
905	5	🚻🛒 🚌 Sakanoshita, Ikeda-pond
906	6	🚌
907	7	🚌 🍴 Hot One, Jizodo
908	8	🚌 ↗ △ (160 m) Leave Route 11 to the right for 1.6 km, hut, bridge, jizo
909	9	🚌 200 m
910	10	🚌 Saifukuji, back on Route 11 for 3 km
911	11	🚌
912	12	🚌 leave Route 11 for 4 km
913	13	Crossing the railway, bridge, Toro stone marker
914	14	🚌 **B12 Enmei-ji,** hut, 🚆 Iyo-Doi, 🛒
915	15	🚌🍴 Sushi
916	16	🚌 pond, back on Route 11
917	17	🚌🍴 Udon 🛒🚻⛩Murayama
918	18	🚌🛒🛒
919	19	
920	20	🚌🍴 Udon
921	21	🚌🚆 Iyo-Sangawa 🍴🛒
922	22	🚌
923	23	🚌🚻🍴
924	24	🚌
925	25	🚌 Henro Goya hut no. 43 🚆 Iyo-Mishima
926	26	🚌 guesthouses in Iyo-Mishima 🛒

Day 45: T65 The Triangle Temple

Distance	20 km
KM	KM 926 to KM 945
🛏	Henro-House Mori-so (KM 938), Minshuku Okada (KM 945)

Today will be only a relaxed walk, with the option of a detour to B13, which would turn our 18 km walk into 26 km. There will be a 4 km climb to T65.

Plan ahead! The convenience store at KM 926 will be the last food store for two days, and there are no restaurants either, and Minshuku Okada is pretty much the only place to stay. In case it is not available, the solution could be to continue for 8 km to Miyoshi or Awa-Ikeda for accommodations. From Miyoshi, it would be 13 km instead of 6 km up to T66 the next day.

KM	Daily km	Point of Interest
	0	🚃 Iyo-Mishima, guesthouses, 🛒
926	1	Turn left, follow Route 11 for 300 m until 🛒
927	2	Several stone markers, pass expressway
928	3	🛈 beginning of climb
929	4	↗ (121 m)
930	5	↓↓
931	6	↗ (200 m)
932	7	↗↗ **T65 Sankaku-ji** △ (354 m) 8.4 km/4 hours detour to **B13**
933	8	(350 m) Panorama point with chairs
934	9	↘ (300 m)
935	10	↘ B13 detour returns to main route, hut
936	11	Monument, Hut (225 m),
937	12	↘ Hut, pass the freeway
938	13	🛏 Henro-House Mori-so (100 m)
939	14	**B14 Jofuku-ji**
940	15	
941	16	🚌 Henro-goya hut No. 37
942	17	🚌 Hichida
943	18	↗ Sakaime Tunnel (length 885 m) Entering Tokushima Prefecture
944	19	End of the tunnel (314 m)
945	20	🚌 Sano, 🛏 Minshuku Okada (282 m)

Day 46: The Highest Point - T66	
Distance	23 km (Challenge: over 900 m climb)
KM	KM 945 to KM 968
🛏	Several options in Kanonji, e. g. Fujikawa Ryokan

Today we will go uphill to the highest point of the pilgrimage near T66. Again, no food or drinks are available on the way.

At T66 we will be leaving Ehime Prefecture, pass Tokushima Prefecture for just 8 km and enter Kagawa Prefecture when reaching T66.

If our legs are too tired, we can take the ropeway down into the valley to protect our knees from the steep walk downhill. The distance from the ropeway station to KM 955 is 3 km walking but the ropeway saves us the very steep downhill part of 800 m decline.

We can even take an easier way, using the ropeway in both directions: From our stay along Route 8 directly to the ropeway station which is 14.5 km with an altitude gain of only 316 m, go up and down to T66 by ropeway, and then continue to Kanonji. That would be 24 km in total – the same distance, but much less altitude to cover.

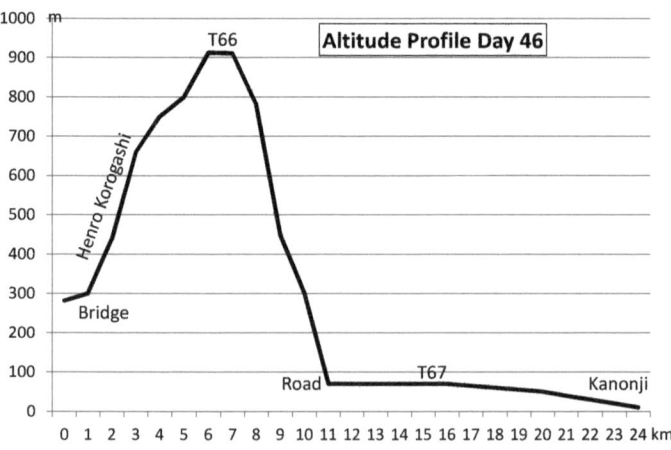

68

KM	Daily km	Point of Interest
945	0	(282 m) Leave Route 192 to the left. Detour to **B15** makes this stage 22 km longer: 45 km. 22 km to B15, stay on Route 192, sleep in Awa-Ikeda
946	1	
947	2	↗↗ (440 m) Henro Korogashi section
948	3	↗ (660 m)
949	4	↗ (750 m)
950	5	↗↗ (800 m) Parking of T66
951	6	↗ **T66 Unpen-ji** △ (912 m), end of detour to B15 🚠 down optional. Lower ropeway station is near B16.
952	7	Entering Kagawa Prefecture (911 m)
953	8	↘↘ (783 m) Detour to **B16** (4.3 km longer)
954	9	↻↘
955	10	↘↘ (300 m) Road from ropeway meets pilgrimage trail, 🍴 Botan Coffee Shop
956	11	🚌 Taniguchi 🛏 Minshuku Aozoraya
957	12	↘ 🚌
958	13	Iwanabe pond, 🛈, end of detour to B16, hut
959	14	Stone markers
960	15	**T67 Daiko-ji**
961	16	
962	17	Cross Route 377, ⛩ Imamiya
963	18	⛩ Koshin-jinja 🚌 Kodachi
964	19	Shinko-in, pass between ponds
965	20	🍴 Udon, pass under expressway, hut
966	21	Stone marker, pass Route 11 🚌 Shussaku ⛩ Wakamiya
967	22	🍴 Udon 🛒
968	23	🚇 Kanonji 🛒

Day 47: The Kanonji Temples and the Giant Coin

Distance	14 km
KM	KM 969 to KM 983
🛏	KM 980 Hoshigawa Inn
	KM 983 Guesthouse Bed n Chill Shippo-ya

Yesterday was tough, so today we will take it easy. In the morning we have time to explore the double-temple of T68+T69, the park, the giant coin and the temples and shrines on the hill nearby, we can stay until noon. After walking 2 km, we can have lunch at Kanakuma Udon, then slowly visit T70 and finish the last 9 km walking until Shippo-ya guesthouse.

KM	Daily km	Point of Interest
968	0	🚆 Kanonji 🛒
969	1	Central Kanonji, Bridge **T68 Jinne-in and T69 Kannon-ji** ⛩ Kotohiki Hachimangu, giant coin
970	2	⛩ Kawakami-shrine, turn left, follow the river
971	3	
972	4	🍱 Kanakuma Mochi and Udon, cross the bridge
973	5	Passing under the railroad
974	6	**T70 Motoyama-ji** 🍱 Komeda's Coffee continue on Route 11 for 1.3 km, 🚌 Motoyama-shogakko-mae
975	7	🚆 1100 m to Motoyama Station 🍱 Sushiro Sushi, O70 Myoon-ji
976	8	🚌 🍱 Udon, Café 🛒
977	9	Pond, 🚌 Michiue 🛒
978	10	Leave Route 11 to the left between the ponds
979	11	Walk parallel to Route 11 🛒
980	12	🚌 500 m to 🚆 Takase Station 🛒 🍱 McDonald's 🛏 Hoshigawa Inn 🛒 Henro-goya hut No. 53
981	13	Stone markers, continue left 🍱 Ramen
982	14	
983	15	🛏 Guesthouse Bed n Chill Shippo-ya 🚆 Mino Station

Day 48: T70 to T75 - Kobo Daishi's Birthplace

Distance	13 km
KM	KM 983 to KM 996
🛏	Several options in Zentsuji: T75 Guesthouse, Kaze-no-kuguru (KM 997), Mikasa-sukasa (KM 999, next to T76)

Today is another shorter walk, but it will be an intensive day. We will visit five temples and especially T71 and T75 deserve a longer stay. The approach to T71 has over 400 steps and the area is mystic, while T75 has plenty of things to see. Allow at least one hour for each of these temples.

There are several options to sleep around Zentsuji. Consider to stay for a second night to visit Kotohira-Shrine, a huge and interesting Shinto location on a hill about 7 km south of Zentsuji, or to detours to B17 and especially B18 (check its Okunoin on the top of the little hill).

The walk is mostly flat, while the approach to T71 is steep but short.

KM	Daily km	Point of Interest
983	0	🛏 Guesthouse Bed n Chill Shippo-ya 🚃 Mino Station
984	1	
985	2	Stone marker, Daishi-do, Fureai Park Mino 🍜 Udon 🚻 🍜 Roadside station, ↗↗
986	3	**T71 Iyadani-ji** △ (221 m), 3.8 km to **B18**
987	4	↻↘
988	5	↘ Pass under the expressway
989	6	Hut, lake 🏞 stone marker, turn right
990	7	**T72 Mandala-ji** 🚻 🍜 Yakiniku 🚌
991	8	**T73 Shusshaka-ji,** back at T72
992	9	🚌
993	10	**T74 Koyama-ji**
994	11	🍜 Ohara Udon, Miyagawa Seimencho Udon
995	12	**T75 Zentsu-ji,** 🚃 Zentsuji, 7 km to Kotohira, 25 km detour to **B17,** 🛏
996	13	🚃 Zentsuji, 🛏

To have enough time to avoid being under pressure, we need to begin our pilgrimage latest at 9:00 a. m.

Day 49: To Sakaide - T76, T77 and T78

Distance	18 km
KM	KM 996 to KM 1013 (Sakaide)
🛏	Several options in Sakaide

We will approach Sakaide, Shikoku's northernmost point. Sakaide is the connecting point of one of the three bridges to Honshu and only point where Shikoku is connected to Honshu by train. This makes it a busy location. The location and bridge can be overlooked from the hill at T78.

The walk is mostly across urban areas. At KM 1013 we will pass the Kamada Museum, the famous building from the 1920's, owned by a major soy sauce company nearby It appears as a library in Haruki Murakami's novel *Kafka at the Beach*.

Full km	Daily km	Point of Interest
996	0	🚉 Zentsuji
997	1	🛏 Kaze-no-kuguru
998	2	Pass under expressway, 🍴 bakery
999	3	**T76 Konzo-ji,** 🍴 Udon Nagata-in Kanoka 🛏 Mikasa-sukasa
1000	4	⛩ Izumo 🛈 🛒
1001	5	
1002	6	600 m to 🚉 Tadotsu, **T77 Doryu-ji**
1003	7	🛒 🍴 Joyfull
1004	8	🚉 Sanuki-Shioya 🍴
1005	9	⛩
1006	10	Henro-goya hut no. 18 🛒 🚉 Marugame, Castle
1007	11	🛒 🛈 Bridge 🍴 Ikkaku
1008	12	🍴 🛒
1009	13	🚉 Utazu 🛒
1010	14	**T78 Gosho-ji** 🛒 ⛩ 🛈 Bridge
1011	15	🛒 Henro-goya hut No. 42 🛈
1012	16	
1013	17	🛈 🚉 Sakaide 🛒
	18	🛏 1-2 km north of the route

Day 50: An Emperor's Grave and T79-T81-T82-T80	
Distance	23 km
KM	KM 1013 to KM 1024 (including a detour to T81 and T82)
🛏	Several options near T80 Kokubu

Today, after visiting T79, we will pick an unconventional route and visit T81 and T82 <u>before</u> staying near T80. We will follow the route of Emperor Sutoku who died in exile at T79 (KM 1016), his body was kept at Yasoba-no-mizu (also at KM 1016) waiting for orders from the capital on how to deal with the ritual of burying an exiled emperor. Finally last he was buried near T81 (KM 1030) but we will not pass his grave, which is slightly northwest of T81, basically on a shortcut to the temple.

T81 and T82 are a high up on the Goshiki-dai plateau (named for its 5 colors), while T80 is in the valley below and has accommodations nearby where we will stay. Today, from KM 1016, we will not follow the popular route but visit the temples in a different order: First to T81, then to T82 and finally downhill to T80 which we can visit tomorrow after breakfast. This used to be a common route as the climb to the plateau is less steep from the west side.

We can also end the day by taking the train to Takamatsu and return and continue from T80 the next day directly to T83.

This is a day with an average distance but it has some tough climbs and descents containing over 500 m of climb over 8 km (average 6-7%)

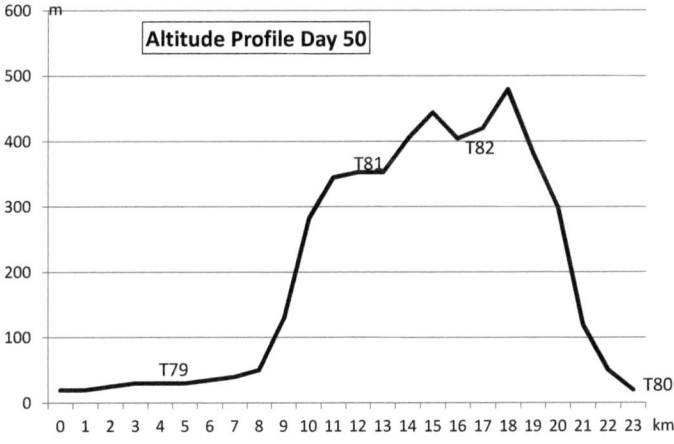

KM	Daily km	Point of Interest
	0	Return to the pilgrimage route
1013	1	🚉 Sakaide
1014	2	Henro-goya Hut No. 41, stone marker, keep right
1015	3	🚇, railroad crossing, Yasoba-no-mizu temple
1016	4	**T79 Tennoji,** ⛩ O79 Shiraminegu, 🚉 Yasoba, turn left (north), cross the railroad for shortcut to T81-T82
	5	Stone marker at the river
Alternate route	6	Ruins of emperor Sutoku's residence
	7	Matsuura-ji, stone markers 🔘 🛈
	8	↗ beginning of climb ⛩ Takaya
	9	↗ (50 m)
	10	↗↗ (130 m) Jizo statues, in the serpentine at the hut leave the road to the left, Emperor's grave, walk along the lanterns uphill for about 600 m
1029	11	**T81 Shiromine-ji** (281 m)
1030	12	↗ Cemetery, O81 Bishamon-kutsu (345 m)
1031	13	(360 m) Akai Well
1032	14	↗↗
1033	15	△ (450 m) Hut 🛈 🔘 Michikusa
1034	16	↘ **T82 Negoro-ji** (404 m) follow Route 180 south
Alternate route	17	(420 m) Henro Goya hut #51 🛈 follow Route 180
	18	↗ (479 m) follow Route 180 south-west
	19	↘ (383 m), turn left, leave Route 180, continue trail south downhill to T80, hut
1026	20	↘↘ (300 m) very steep downhill parts
1025	21	↘ hut 🛈 (120 m) cemetery
1024	22	↘ (50 m)
1023	23	**T80 Kokubun-ji** 🛏
1024	24	🚉 Kokubu

Day 51: T80, T83 and into Takamatsu	
Distance	16 km
KM	KM 1024 to KM 1054 (shortcut avoiding T81 and T82)
🛏	Many options in Takamatsu

As we visited T81 and T82 with plenty of climbs yesterday, we can continue directly from T80 (Kokubunji) to T83. Today will be smooth: We will be walking 500 m south, along the pond, cross Route 11 and turn left when we hit Route 12. After staying on that road for 9 km (we can walk one block south parallel to it after 5 km) we will reach T83. After visiting T83 and the shrine next to it, we will finish the day in Takamatsu. It will be a flat walk of only 16 km with no time pressure.

T83 is located on the southern end of Takamatsu. We can spend at least two nights in Takamatsu and walk parts of T83 to T86 every day, before proceeding to T88 and finishing the pilgrimage.

KM	Daily km	Point of Interest
Alternate route	0	**T80 Kokubunji,** go 500 m south along Sekinoike-pond, cross Route 11, turn left on Route 12
	1	🍽 Jizo-statue 🛒
	2	🛒
	3	↗
	4	↘ Henjo-In, Mikuriya Pond
	5	
	6	🛒
	7	🍽 Udon, bridge
	8	
1047	9	Henro-goya hut No. 24, **T83 Ichinomiya-ji** 🚌
1048	10	🚌 🛒
1049	11	
1050	12	🍽 Sushi 🛒
1051	13	Hut, ℹ️, YouMe Town shopping center 🍽 Yoshinoya 🚊 Sanjo
1052	14	
1053	15	🚊 Ritsurin 🚊 Kawaramachi
1054	16	🚊 Central Takamatsu

Day 52: Takamatsu: T84, T85 and T86

Distance	20 km
KM	KM 1053 to KM 1072
🛏	Many options in Takamatsu, guesthouses near T86

The next three temples are near Takamatsu, we can walk our backpack and return to our accommodation at night by public transportation if we want.

T84 and T85 are two amazing temples both situated on steep hills, overlooking the sea. The walk is challenging with two short steep climbs. Back on sea level we will continue along the coast to T86 which is next to a train station.

KM	Daily km	Point of Interest
	0	Central Takamatsu
1053	1	🚉 Ritsurin
1054	2	Central Takamatsu, 🚉 Kawaramachi
		🚉 every 500 to 1000 m for the next 4 km
1055	3	🏖 🚉 Oki-matsushima
1056	4	🏖 🚉 Kasugagawa
1057	5	🏖 🚉 Katamoto
1058	6	🚉 Kotoden Yashima, bus shuttle to T84
		Hut 🏠, lakes, beginning of climb
1059	7	↗↗ Yashima Okajisui temple,
		Kuwazuno-nashi temple
1060	8	↗↗ **T84 Yashima-ji** △ (286 m) 🚌 to 🚉 Katamoto
1061	9	↘↘
1062	10	↘↘ turn right at the foot of the hill,
		Gempei war memorials
1063	11	Cross the bridge, 🚉 Yakuri (500 m south)
1064	12	↗↗
1065	13	↗
1066	14	↗↗ **T85 Yakuri-ji** △ (229 m) ↘
1067	15	↘
1068	16	↘ Hut 🏠
1069	17	
1070	18	🚉 Shioya 🚉 Fusazaki, Aizen-ji 🍜 Udon, hut, ⛩
1071	19	🚉 Hara O86 Jizoji 🏖 hut
1072	20	**T86 Shido-ji,** 🚉 Shido, 🚌 to T87 and 88

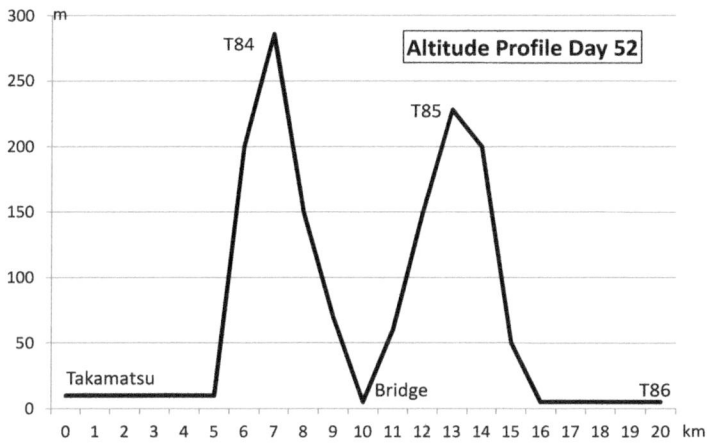

Looking down over Takamatsu from T84

L

Day 53 : The Final Temples: T87 and T88

Distance	20 km (Challenge!)
KM	KM 1072 to KM 1092
🛏	Return to Takamatsu by bus, or stay at Yasokubo near T88

Today's stage will take us to the last temples of the pilgrimage. We will continue where we stopped yesterday and walk from the seaside into the mountains to an altitude of about 740 m, with a steep part towards the end, in case we follow the traditional route.

To follow the traditional route, make sure to turn right instead of crossing the bridge after 5 km, continue until the hut and cross Kabe river at the hut. We will have a longer rest at KM 1085, when we will take a break at the Henro Salon next to the lake, visit the pilgrimage museum and collect our completion certificate. From here we chose between

- an easier but longer route to T88 (Route C in the Route Guide), or
- a short but steep route (the most popular one, Route B), or
- a detour to B20 (also starting with Route C).

Route A and B are mostly the same except the first 4 km from Nagao.

After visiting T88, we can return by bus to Shido station, but beware: The last bus leaves at 4 pm. In order to reach T88 early enough, around 3 pm, we should begin our hike at T86 before 8 am. Instead, we can stay next to T88 at Yasukubo guesthouse, if it is available.

KM	Daily km	Point of Interest
1072	0	�# **T86 Shido-ji,** 🚆 Shido, follow Route 3, cross Route 11
1073	1	🛣 pass under expressway
1074	2	🚏 Shido bus stop, Osayuki-pond 🚆 Orange-town
1075	3	⛩
1076	4	O87 Gyokusenji, 🛣 🍽 Udon, Ramen
1077	5	Route 3 becomes Route 37, old stone marker, turn right BEFORE the bridge, walk 300 m along graveyard until hut, cross Kabe river on henro bridge
1078	6	Old road marker 50 m left ⛩ 🍽 Café Pause
1079	7	Turn right to **T87 Nagao-ji,** 🚆 🚏 Nagao ⛩ 🛏 InnTek-Tek 🛣 🍽 Ramen
1080	8	Cross Kabe river again 🛣
1081	9	Hosei-ji
1082	10	Taka-Jizo 🚏 Ichin-ji

1083	11	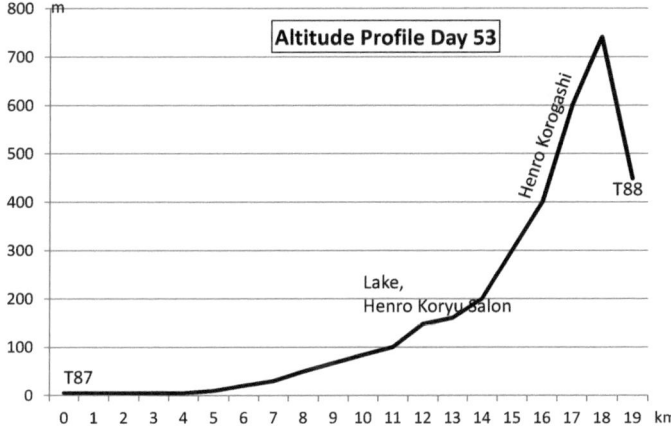 Oishi-jinja
1084	12	Shimo-Nakazu, stone marker Oishi
1085	13	Hut, Maeyama village, Ohenro-Koryu-salon (Pilgrimage Museum) lake (148 m), decide between different routes. Easier way to T88 (4 km longer, route C) and partly challenging popular way with more climb (Route A & B), or appr. 15 km to B20 (also begin with Route C)
1086	14	Gion-shrine Kurusu
1087	15	(160 m)
1088	16	↗ (226 m) hut
1089	17	↗
1090	18	↗↗ (452 m) Henro korogashi
1091	19	↗↗ Henro korogashi △ (741 m) hut, O88 Taizo-mine
1092	20	↘↘ **T88 Okubo-ji** (448 m) appr. 14.3 km to **B20**

The distance from Maeyama village to T88 via B20 is 29 km longer and cannot be managed on foot in one day. Unfortunately, there are no accommodations nearby so B20 cannot easily be visited on foot due to lack of accommodations.

This is not the end of the pilgrimage, as we will return to T1 where we started.

79

Day 54: Back to Tokushima Pref. - T88 to T10

Distance	20 km
KM	KM 1093 – KM 30 (Alternative Route)
⛏	Henro-House HS Japan, 3 km from T10 or GH Yawata

If we stayed in Shido or Takamatsu, we can return up to T88 by bus. The earliest bus leaves from JR Shido at 7:50 and arrives at T88 at 9:12. If we take the first bus, we can still make it to T10 before sunset. This is an easy walk which takes us mostly downhill on paved roads.

This stage, starting from T88, is just 21 km to T10 on the other side of the mountain range and a little further to our accommodation. It is a beautiful hike mostly downhill and it is a little bit shorter than the popular route from T88 to T1.

There are several other possibilities to connect T88 to Tokushima Prefecture, e. g. by returning to Takamatsu or T86, to follow the north coast to Sanuki-aioi station for 30 km and to cross the hills to T3 (17 km).

KM	Daily km	Point of Interest
1093	0	**T88 Okuboji** (448 m) ↘ Follow route 377 eastwards for 5 km
1094	1	↘ (306 m)
1095	2	↘ Jizodo temple
1096	3	↘ (250 m) Gomyo tunnel
1097	4	
1098	5	↘ After the tunnel, turn right, follow Route 2 south, entering Tokushima Prefecture
1099	6	↘ ⛏ Uta Guesthouse (218 m)
Alternative Route	7	↘ 🍴 Gyoza, sunflower field
	8	↘ (191 m) 🚻 hut
	9	↘ ⛩ Shinmeisha 🍴
	10	(120 m) 🚻
	11	🍴 Ramen restaurant
	12-14	
	15	🚦 Turn left at the traffic light ⛏ Brompton Lodge 600m
	16	🚦 Kamigirai-Bridge, continue straight
	17	
	18	🍴 Turn left onto Road 139 at Awa City Hall
	19	🚻 🍴 **T10 Kirihata-ji** ⛏ Henro House HS Japan
	20	🍴 ⛏ Guesthouse Yawata

Day 55: Completing the Circle: Back to T1

Distance	Km 1094 (Alternate Route)
Km	Henro-House HS Japan, 3 km from T10

This is the last day of our pilgrimage. We will return to Temple No. 1 and collect a return-stamp which is put on a separate page in our stamp book.

It will be the reverse walk of our first 2 days. If we skip all the temples and go straight to T1, it is appr. 20 km following Route 12, or 28 km including returns to all the temples from T9 to T1. Collecting stamps at these temples means we are already starting our second round of the pilgrimage.

The route including the return temple visits is described here, the nicest route is to follow the traditional henro way along the places of worship on Route 139.

After completing the loop and revisiting T1, many pilgrims complete their pilgrimage with a visit to Koyasan, which has a special page in our stamp book.

KM	Daily km	Point of Interest
30	0	Henro-goya hut no. 4, 🍴 Guesthouse Yawata Return to Route 139, 1 km north ⛩ Wakamiya Hachimangu
27	1	(optional 2 km detour to T10) Shonen-ji ⛩ Hiyoshishinmei shrine stone marker ⛩ Ebisu shrine
26	2	Bridge, turn right, Azukiarai-daishi, enko-ji, daishi statue
25	3	Stone marker, **T9 Horinji** 🍴
24	4	Turn right, stone marker
23	5	Turn right 🍴 Yakitori, pass under expressway Nyomon gate ⛩ Pond
22	6	
21	7	Henro Goya hut no. 27 🛈 stone marker
20	8	🛏 Henro House Okudaya, Meki Daishi
19	9	Bridge, Kannon-an
18	10	**T7 Juraku-ji,** stone marker
17	11	**T6 Anraku-ji** 🚍 Higashihara
16	12	🚍 Kajiyabara

15	13	🍲 Udon, Bridge ⛩ ⛩
14	14	🍲 Udon 🚌 Kanyake (300 m)
13	15	Hut
12	16	🏕 🍲 ♨ 🚌 Rakan
		T5 Jizo-ji
11	17	O5 Gohyaku-rakan
10	18	🏕 ⛩
9	19	**T4 Dainichi-ji**
8	20	O3 Aizen-in
7	21	
6	22	Hokoku-ji ⛩ Suwa-jinja 🚃
5 or 1133	23	Hut, 🚃 Itano,
4 or 1134	24	**T3 Konsenji**
3 or 1135	25	🚃 Awa-Kawabata
2 or 1136	26	**T2 Gokuraku-ji**
1 or 1137	27	**T1 Ryozenji,** 🚃 Bando

From T1, we can walk to Bando station and take the train back to Tokushima or walk to Naruto-east bus station at the expressway and take a bus to Osaka or another major city.

If you feel like staying in a quiet pilgrimage environment, you may consider to walk the Shodoshima pilgrimage (88 small temples on the Island of Shodoshima), this takes a bit less than 2 weeks, the island is 3 hours from Takamatsu by ship.

Another very popular pilgrimage is the Shinto-related Kumano-kodo on the southern tip of the Kii peninsula, south of Osaka, with distances of 70 to 160 km depending on the route.

Preface 5

Day 0 - Arrival in Tokushima 8

Day 1: T1 to T6 - The Start (by Train to Bando) 9

Day 2: T7 to T10 and Crossing Yoshino River 10

Day 3: T11 and T12 - Heavy Duty 12

Day 4: T13 to T17 and back to Tokushima City 14

Day 5: T18 and T19 - Leaving the City 16

Day 6: T20 and T21 - Two Tough Beauties 17

Day 7: T22 and T23 - To the Coast 19

Day 8: T23 to T24 Part 1: Sleeping on a Tiny Island ... 21

Day 9: T23 to T24 Part 2 – The End of the Railroad ... 23

Day 10: T23 to T24 Part 3 - The Sky and the Sea 24

Day 11: T24, T25, T26 and Cape Muroto 26

Day 12: From Kiragawa to Nahari 27

Day 13: From Nahari to Aki including T27 28

Day 14: From Aki to T28 - Approaching Kochi 29

Day 15: T29 and T30 - Entering Kochi 30

Day 16: T31 - T32 - T33 - Leaving Kochi 31

Day 17: T34 and T35 - Across the Flatlands 32

Day 18: T36 to T37 Part 1 - Usa to Susaki................................. 33

Day 19: T36 to T37 Part 2 - from Susaki to Tosa-Kure 35

Day 20: T36 to T37 Part 3 - from Tosa-Kure to T37.................. 36

Day 21: T37 to T38 Part 1 – From Kubokawa to Cape Ino........ 38

Day 22: T37 to T38 Part 2 - Cape Ino to Nakamura................. 40

Day 23: T37 to T38 Part 3 - From Nakamura to Okinohama 41

Day 24: T37 to T38 Part 4 – The Cape, at Last! 42

Day 25: T38 to T39 Part 1 - Back to Okinohama 44

Day 26: T38 to T39 Part 2 – Forests and Rivers 45

Day 27: T38 to T39 Part 3 - T39 and Sukumo 46

Day 28: Half-Time at T40.. 47

Day 29: Along the West Coast 48

Day 30: From Tsushima to Uwajima 49

Day 31: T41 - T42 - T43: Three in a Row!.................................. 50

Day 32: T43 to T44 Part 1 – Unomachi to Ozu......................... 51

Day 33: T43 to T44 Part 2 – A Famous Bridge 52

Day 34: T43 to T44 Part 3 – Into the Mountains....................... 53

Day 35: T43 to T44 Part 4 – To Kuma-Kogen 54

Day 36: The Loop to T45 and back... 55

Day 37: Leaving the Mountains to T46 57

Day 38: T47 to T51 - Entering Matsuyama 58

Day 39: T52 and T53 - Leaving Matsuyama 59

Day 40: T54 and T55 - To the Northwestern Cape 60

Day 41: T56 to T59 and to Nyugawa 62

Day 42: A Tough Day - T60 to T62 63

Day 43: Straight and Flat - T62 - T63 - T64 65

Day 44: Along the Inland Sea to Iyo-Mishima 66

Day 45: T65 The Triangle Temple 67

Day 46: The Highest Point - T66 68

Day 47: The Kanonji Temples and the Giant Coin 70

Day 48: T70 to T75 - Kobo Daishi's Birthplace 71

Day 49: To Sakaide - T76, T77 and T78 72

Day 50: An Emperor's Grave and T79-T81-T82-T80 73

Day 51: T80, T83 and into Takamatsu 75

Day 52: Takamatsu: T84, T85 and T86 76

Day 53 :The Final Temples: T87 and T88 78

Day 54: Back to Tokushima Pref. - T88 to T10 80

Day 55: Completing the Circle: Back to T1 81

Notes: